GOD WITHIN US:

Movements, Powers, and Joys

by Peter A. Fraile, S.J.

Loyola University Press
Chicago 60657

Loyola University Press
3441 North Ashland Avenue
Chicago, Illinois 60657

All biblical quotations are taken from *The Jerusalem Bible: Reader's Edition* with the permission of the publisher, Doubleday and Company.

Library of Congress Cataloging in Publication Data
Fraile, Peter A., 1937–
    God within us.
    Includes index.
    1. Spiritual life—Catholic authors. I. Title.
BX2350.2.F69 1986   248.4'82   86-2871
ISBN 0-8294-0503-8

The living God.... chooses to come close to the human being and embrace his people . . . in the embrace of becoming one, assuming back into himself what first by creation came from him, and giving to the humanbeing a second gift greater than the first of creation. This second gift is sonship and an astonishing union which raise without measure the dignity of the human to divine levels.

from "The Joy of Discovering
the Living God,"
Peter A. Fraile, S.J.

Contents

Acknowledgment

I see what is written as an attempt to describe what I feel as the beginning of a process whose dimensions go much beyond me.

I am grateful to the God who gently and powerfully is the source and ultimate reason of this fascinating movement of existing.

I am grateful to Jesus of Nazareth, whom I feel still in us and with us and who clearly mirrors and is the uplifting movement of divinizing what is human and who unites this movement with that other of God's humanization, God's incarnation and self-expression.

I'm grateful to God's and Jesus' Spirit who, given to us and living in us, inspires, energizes, enlightens, and creates immeasurable forces of love, union, and hope.

I'm grateful to those who believe, hope and love me; without you the path would be most difficult and senseless. Grateful and indebted to participants in the "Divine and Human" workshops, because your listening helps me talk, your asking helps me give, your presence helps me see.

I'm grateful specifically to so many of you in unique and ineffable ways.

Daring to be the speaker for us all, it is proper for me to express here as well our gratitude to Denise Anderson and Barbara Liegl for the collaboration, enthusiasm, and physical arrangement of this book.

Peter

Introduction:

A Vision

A vision keeps me going through the years: a good vision, a sacred one. Life itself gave it to me; it is growing and is the horizon of my existing. Amazingly, it is coming true.

My vision is not a sleeping dream but a waking one. The more it takes hold of me, the more awake I become. It is about life, and you and me, and all people, and the universe, and God, and the past, the future, and especially the present. I dream of harmony, union, everything fitting together, a oneness evolving yet already here.

The vision is hard to express but easy to grasp, because we are in it. You see how the fingers of the hand are many, but integrated into one hand. The hand is the whole, the fingers are parts, perfectly united and harmonized. Indeed, there is a wealth of examples that many form a one, that the one holds the many together in a new entity which gives meaning to the many. Thus we, the many—people and other things or beings in the universe—form one; the one holds us together, integrates us, and we become a new entity in it. The one is an expression of and comes from another still greater one whom we call God.

Dreams, living dreams, are good. Merely by hints, suggestions, and foreshadowing, they present many possibilities, and explain much. They are the dimension of hope, the open horizon of being. They are also fun to share; many people will say: "that is my dream as well." What surprises me is that this dream has a symmetrical aspect: it is the same looking forward as backward, upward or downward, to the right or to the left; it is spherical.

The center is God; in him everything and every dimension integrates. He is the one, the total one, living; in him we all become one, a new entity, a beautiful reality. In him we move, are, and exist; he is, moves, and exists in us. We are different realities but so marvelously connected that the result is another greater reality, that mysterious one, greater than we, which is the source of our energy, meaning, beauty, and becoming.

The dream is real. The dream is here. We are in it. It is light. It is energy. It makes sense. It is powerful. It belongs to all of us. It is us. Living it is more enjoyable than dreaming it. It is like a gift from the whole to the parts, from the one to the many.

Do you realize what it is to live without a living dream? Sometimes I wonder how much we as groups or societies need such a dream, and what happens when we lose it. My inner answer comes in a nightmare vision of confusion, anxiety, despair, fighting for a position to be in, elbowing, envy, jealousy, and all those ugly perspectives and feelings. More or less that is what happens to me when I chance to lose my integrating dream.

I am learning how to gently listen to my overall sacred and all-encompassing dream. It is there. I let it talk to me, it organizes my perspective of life, even my emotions and feelings; also, it offers a governor, an automatic switch control for actions and life courses.

Listening to a life dream is like listening to God. The dream is outside yet from within; it is itself a word, a light; looking into it is inspiring, enlightening, unleashes forces of being. Of course, some of these dreams can be, and many are, delusions. But there is a great difference between a real dream and a delusory one. The real one is permanent, gentle, consistent, peaceful, and strong. It integrates everything, is open to test; its roots go deep even beyond one's own roots, its scope embraces all life. In general, it is a harmonizing force; contemplation of it is life-giving and generates enthusiasm and joy. The delusory dream is generally noted for its inconsistence, anxiety, short life span, contradictions, partiality, fears of being discovered and destroyed. It is more temporary and partial, has tones of selfishness, and grows on insecurity.

Tuning into a positive real life dream is like sensing a call to be; it is the expansion of self and the experience of a phenomenon of order, cosmic order. It is like entering into a universal flow of unity. My God is a God of unity, a unity that perhaps we humans have not yet begun to grasp. I feel that if someone could properly express this unity as the horizon of our common existing, the expression would be so powerful and exciting that it would inevitably create a revolution. I also feel that the time is ripe for such a vision and that we all are longing for it. The sketching of such vision would turn a floodlight on the path for which we are all searching with tiny tapers.

Jesus of Nazareth did that; he opened human existence to eternity with the proclamation of our divine sonship and the introduction of the fact of resurrection and the continuity of life for ever. Sometimes I wonder whether the message got diverted into religious practices good in themselves but disconnected from the total great vision of our eternal dimension, the perspective of oneness with our God.

My life dream is: the coming to be of the one, oneness at many levels—self, social, and cosmic, inner and outer oneness with my God. Integration of the parts—myself and everything—with the whole, God. The totally harmonized movement that is peace. Proper evolving into greater and higher existence.

The perception and perspective of the dream itself fit goals to vision and energize movement towards the goals. For the dream is the grasping of life's direction and the inner reasons to be. It is a mystical opening into my being and the total being. Perhaps I should not have called it a vision or dream, because in fact it is too realistic to be a dream. Nonetheless, it is essentially incomplete; it has the characteristics of a dream: projection into the future and sketchiness.

If I can keep my dream alive, my sense of direction is stable; I will have a constant source of inspiration, a channel of energy integration, and the prophetic dimension of my own life will be fulfilled. That is an energy reservoir. Moreover, I feel that our communities and our national and international societies hope to reawaken some similar dream endowed with the power to direct, unite, and resurrect. Yes, who does not hope for life? Who would not delight in a clear horizon and perspective? Who would refuse the joy of a profitable and overwhelmingly sound return on self-investment? The vision and dream of oneness is not only possible but guaranteed by our God, the God of union, the God of oneness.

I am talking about not just a message to be delivered, or a doctrine to be preached; it is a mysterious reality to be enjoyed, lived, and generously shared.

The dream is not mine; I encountered it first in Jesus of Nazareth, the Christ, the anointed one sent by God with the liberating message of our eternal oneness as the central process of being and becoming.

God, we need a dream to live from, a worthwhile dream to live for. We also need prophets to clarify that dream for all of us, to speak it out and verbalize it for the rest of us to know and see. It is obvious that life is a journey somewhere; we would like to see where we are going.

Part 1

Discovering the Living God

The Joy of Discovering the Living God

I thought that God was far away or beyond the clouds. Gradually I discovered that my God is a living God, living in people and in me. Suddenly the lives of others and my life acquired another meaning, a divine dimension that is overwhelmingly beautiful and non-threatening. This is not a delusion because I experience in it none of the characteristics of delusion. The experience does not come from me but from the very core and reality of life.

The living God humbly incarnated himself in people and in life, because he so wanted. This is not pantheism but a manifestation of a loving God, who because he loves and essentially is love, chooses to come close to the human being and embrace his people—his children—in the embrace of becoming one, assuming back into himself what first by creation came from him, and giving to the human being a second gift greater than the first of creation. This second gift is sonship and an astonishing union which raise without measure the dignity of the human to divine levels.

I am not talking about an ideal or a possible hypothesis, or an abstract concept; what I am talking about is an experience of something much greater than the experience. God lives among us in a perceptible way; otherwise, his communication would not be proper, nor perfect. We have the right and the obligation to perceive his presence and feel his action, and to adore, accept, and respond to his gifting of himself.

Incarnation—the process of God becoming human and thus dignifying humankind—is a gift greater than creation and the giving of life, because in this process the giver himself is the gift, and we become one with the one from whom we come.

Blessed are those who can perceive and taste the reality of a living God among us and within us.

Perhaps relating to an abstract ideological God is easier for the human being because one can have some control on the relating. We can manipulate our ideas and concepts. However, the excitement, wonder, and dimensions of relating to a living incarnated God are beyond telling. Suddenly life and being take on a dimension of truth which is like comparing talking about food and eating, fantasizing about love and being in love. The images are a poor shadow though, because we cannot compare God and the depths of his reality to anything.

Crossing Through Barriers

It is a great blessing to cross that ideological barrier; the relationship becomes different, reality is other. Perhaps as in air travel, there is a so-called sound barrier, at other levels of our being there are many other barriers, and there is an idealogical barrier that does not allow us to break free from our concepts and intellectual constructs. But we can learn to cross the barriers, and thus liberate ourselves from constraints that bind our perceptions and the expansive forces of our own nature.

Unlearning and Liberating of Self

The quieting of the contemplative and the mystic allows the inner mystical forces to emerge and diminishes resistance, and thus makes it easier to cross thought and feeling boundaries towards new horizons of experience. It is a task of liberation from self; sometimes, a process of unlearning. Religious education at these levels has to be an education to the freedom of inner forces instead of binding us with ideas.

Can it be that God lives in me and others? Do I have any right to deny it?

Should I relate to a philosophical concept of God or to a living God? If I accept that God lives in me and I live in him, would my attitudes, feelings, and meaningfulness be different?

Jesus of Nazareth believed that a living God, whom he calls Father, was in him and they became one.

Jesus' dream and desire was that we become one with God as he did. This was his message, the good news. Can we accept a living God within us? St. Paul says: "In God we live and move and exist." (Acts 17:28.) We can say as well that God lives, moves, and exists in us.

Such reality, if accepted, changes many of our attitudes. We can no longer place very much importance on ourselves in the sense of our temporal being. Perhaps we are reluctant to do that. We do not realize that by giving up our little selfishness we acquire the greatness of God.

A Symphony of Movements

I wonder at and like the symphony of movements that I see in Jesus of Nazareth. There is a prayer and desire within me to enter into the same symphony and become part of it. Not only does it seem possible, but perhaps we are made to exist and become within those movements.

The movements of a vehicle determine its coordinates, direction, and even existential relationships. For example, an automobile is a combination of movements both within itself and in relation to people and distances. When its movements are healthy and well orchestrated, the vehicle becomes most meaningful and enjoyable, it blends with and enhances the life of its rider.

Thus the movement of a person, both inner and in relation to surrounding life can be and are meant to be orchestrated; then they generate life, joy, and meaning; they enhance being.

In Jesus of Nazareth I see movements: inner movements in relation to himself, his identity, and self-perception; movements towards people and the world; movements towards his God and life—clear movements that make much sense and open a great perspective of being for many of us.

I find in myself and others a natural great longing for harmony of movements and a joy in such harmony. That is a healthy longing: the greater the harmony, the greater both the enthusiasm for life and the sense of well-being.

Human movements can be categorized in many ways. They can be physical, emotional, psychological, existential, spiritual. They can be personal-individual, social-organizational, even cosmic. According to their effects, they can be healthy or unhealthy, constructive or destructive, joyful or painful, senseless or meaningful. Most of them interrelate and are interdependent.

What I would like to develop in me is what I perceive in Jesus of Nazareth: a sense of order and priority, the maintenance of essential movements which will get me where I want to be, and which will keep the healthy dynamism of my becoming what I am and what I am supposed to be.

The first most important movement, as I can see, is the one that points me towards the main goal: the eternity of my being, the assurance of a continuation of worthwhile life, my incorporation with the total being, a good life insurance. If this movement and direction is cleared, all other movements can be better managed.

Note that talking about these movements implies a dynamic concept of the human being, in which stability is not stagnation, but is precisely a balance of moving and meaningful change. Thus security and health are felt only in the process itself of moving and changing.

The monitoring of movements is naturally important; there are easy ways to find out when we are stagnant or moving, when we approach danger, when the speed and steering are right, when refueling is needed. We have traffic signs and automatic feedback monitors which tell us where we are and how we are doing. We have too, in all areas of our being, experts who can advise us of conditions and recommend repairs.

I am going towards an eternal and fulfilled life which I would like to be insured. So far, the best definition and experience of such life is given by Jesus, a man that found God and made the best alliance with his God—sonship and oneness. He says that I can enter into the same plan of being and cut the trail. Following him and his path or policy, I would be okay. I have already signed the policy; therefore, I should probably enjoy it.

Within this policy, the energy is provided for by his God, who is my God, with no restrictions except those which I make. The energy is the Spirit and life of that God who willingly offers to come and dwell in me.

With this fuel and energy, I must undertake to use

them efficiently, and try to move and function properly with them.

The Spirit—life—of my God in me, by itself produces great movements of oneness in love, security in faith, freedom in being, becoming in hope, and expansiveness in sharing. If I can manage to remove obstacles and eliminate restrictions, then I will be sailing with good winds.

God of Movement

God, you are a God of movement, that is of life and creation, you are the God of the living, not the God of the dead. You, like creation, are the permanent becoming of everything and everybody. You are not a God of stagnation, arteriosclerosis, or paralysis, but the opposite: a God who calls to life and joy, who gives life and joy.

Yes, you are a pleasant God and an exciting God. In your presence we feel the forces of creation; what was not comes into being; you are to us what spring is to the earth. Your movements are beautiful and not threatening. You move towards us with fatherly love and understanding, with the open arms of a friend. A friendly God you are. You tell us not to fear but to trust. And you move us by invitation and grace to be your children, to love and unite with you. How lucky we are to exist from you, in you and to you.

Jesus told us about you, he called you *Abba*, and he described to us your intentions and attitudes, your boundless goodness and mercy, your loving essence, your powerful gentleness. You are the God that in Christ raises people from death to life, makes the blind see and deaf hear, makes cripples walk and the unloving love. You move towards us your people with gentleness, forgiveness, peace, plenty of gifts, and a father's longing for union.

There are other movements in our being;

sometimes we feel and suffer such movements like fear, separation, lack of life, and death; unholy movements enter at times into us, individually and socially. We are subject to evil. It is no surprise that at times we feel afraid and anxious.

Knowing all that, we can appreciate you more. We need you, God of goodness greater than the evil that haunts us. You tell us not to fear, that you are with us and will always be. Living with you is incomparably much better than without you. Knowing you, who would like to be far from you?

I wish I could know you more like Jesus did, then I would love you more and you would be in me; I would be truly alive. "This is eternal life, to know you, the only true God." (Jn 17:3.)

Move me in your movements. I want to be your image, and I want you to be where I live, so that others may see you in me, appreciate the movements of respect, peace, compassion, truthfulness, of pure and simple goodness.

I know that you want that too.

Here I am, God, I am yours. As Jesus prayed, I humbly want to be one with you. And this desire comes from you. I feel wonderfully blessed.

The Movements of God

When you use a tape recorder, you can see a needle flicker back and forth, or a light brighten and dim as the sound reaches or leaves the best range of volume for recording. When you drive a car, you can monitor speed, fuel and oil levels, keep automatically at the speed limit, and check the functioning of other systems.

Can we monitor the movements of the Spirit in a person, the presence and action of God? Should we? Why would we? For the same reasons that we monitor other activities and functions. To know, to direct, to establish the *status quo*, to determine what we need and where we are, to enjoy a healthy process of being.

How can we monitor God in us?

Where God is and where he is moving, there are perceptible signs of his presence and action. His presence is active and effective.

Ignatius Loyola and other spiritual fathers developed ways to discern and monitor the movements of the spirit in individuals. With such help, I know when I am moved in one direction or another, and ordinarily with what intensity.

Being alert to God's movements is certainly most helpful for spiritual growth. I sense the pulse of a constant movement towards God in the veins of my being which directs and shapes my life; I hope this will always be true. I know it will, as far as God is concerned. I hope that I will respond alertly.

When the pulse is clearer and stronger, I feel that something or someone lives in me and is certainly more consistent than myself. It reminds me of what St. Paul wrote: "I live now not with my own life, but with the life of Christ who lives in me." (Gal 2:20.) St. Teresa of Avila writes,

> I live, yet no true life I know,
> And, living thus expectantly,
> I die because I do not die.
> Since this new death-in-life I've known
> Estranged from self my life has been,
> For now I have a life unseen. . . .

Such presence affects very deeply one's identity; one feels good about it.

My response should be acceptance, adoration, recognition, and immersion into that reality which is in me. It is a gift, a grace, a blessing; it makes me my authentic self, free from self-centeredness. The warm embrace of total being produces a gentle and powerful sense of belonging. It is a deep, inner consolation, a joy so gentle and soothing that one would like to feel that way forever.

Again, the awareness of truth is so clear that there is no possibility of doubt.

The movements of my God include his presence, order, creation, love, life, forgiveness, and the overall movement of being and oneness.

The utmost of movement is quietness and union. The movement of God towards his people and creation is eternal, and goes beyond our concepts of time. That means that my God always loved and loves me, always is and was coming towards me, by his very essence as creator and Father. It is a constant and steady coming and self-giving.

My movement towards him, and mankind's movement towards him, is another question.

Jesus understood, felt, allowed, and submitted himself to God's movement towards him. The result was total oneness. "Father, may they be one in us, as you are in me and I am in you." (Jn 17:21.) "And eternal life is this: to know you, the only true God, and Jesus Christ whom you have sent." (Jn 17:3.) The process of incarnation is the human embodiment of God. It is God and man becoming one in the person of Jesus. It is the process of union between the divine and the human which divinizes humankind and redeems it. Jesus was the firstborn in such process and we are supposed to continue it. That is, to continue accepting God's coming, cooperating with the oneness phenomenon, submitting ourselves to transformation that such phenomenon will generate in us. Eventually it will bring us to resurrection.

God in himself according to what we know is movement. Life in itself is movement. A movement of oneness and love. The trinitarian explanation is movement: the generative movement from the Father to the Son, the returning, glorifying movement from the Son to the Father, the unifying, bonding movement between both of them of the Holy Spirit. Such movements extend themselves towards us, because we too are created, generated, and we can return and glorify, and we are united and bonded.

God is a dynamic reality without which neither life nor ourselves can be explained. Receptivity to God's movements is a salvific and a most healthy spiritual attitude.

The abandonment that mystics talk about must be related to that receptivity and flexibility to being moved by God's initiatives and influence. This was Jesus' attitude of doing the Father's will.

The movements of greatness, proper of a God is shown in the mercifulness and forgiveness characteristic of his way of loving—uniting.

The movement of the great is humility; the one who is great is humble, does not boast, and does not try to be great. His or her greatness is shown in the ability to make himself or herself small and unassuming.

The one who knows does not need to talk too much. The greatness of knowledge and understanding is shown most often in silence and admiration.

The greatness of love embraces everything, perfection and imperfection, light and darkness, right and wrong, good and evil. Thus God loves the just and the sinner, the perfect and the imperfect, what is and what is not, what is past and is to come.

The greatness of speech is saying without saying. Thus there is silent music and the surrounding silence. The greatness of being is not having to prove it, it is being able not to show that one is. God does not need to prove that he is, and the one who is feels peaceful and not anxious about being.

Jesus accepted and admired his Father living in him; consequently he could live from inside out the greatness of his God, the Father. He could see beyond sin, and forgive, he could be beyond structures and regulations, and establish a greater order and the principles of all regulations, that is, love and life. His vision, his feelings, his attitudes, his compassion, his security, his faithfulness and generosity show the greatness of a God.

The Fatherhood-Motherhood Movement

"To have seen me is to have seen the Father." (Jn 14:9.)

Growing up means a transition from childhood to adulthood. Adults exercise the responsibilities of fathering and mothering their children.

Caring for is a father-mother movement.

In the gospel narratives, I see Jesus caring for the disciples: "love one another as I have loved you." (Jn 15:12.) He cares for the sick and the masses. Somehow he exercises a fatherhood-motherhood. This is a relating movement.

Can we, should we assume this movement too? Do we overemphasize within Christianity the child movement of dependency, being taken care of, submission, obedience, and the like, which are good but only one side of being? Could we or should we also guide ourselves to be grown-up Christians and take the role of father, incarnating the fatherhood-motherhood attitude and movement towards the community and one another? I do not mean control but caring and service. I believe we can and we should. It is taking also the posture of the father in the Parable of the Prodigal Son. Perhaps this is one of the aspects of spiritual fatherhood-motherhood.

"If you have seen me you have seen the Father" (Jn 14:9): his mercy, forgiveness, care, love, peacefulness, providence, life-giving warmth. "I am in the Father and the Father is in me." (Jn 14:10.)

The Movement of Jesus towards Others

Self-centering and what I call navel-gazing, when

it happens to be exaggerated, is a considerable obstacle to spiritual growth and development. It may become an obsession with self, and entail open and hidden fears and insecurities.

The expansive movement of unselfishness, the switch of the object of concern and consciousness from self to others and then God, is opposed to a self-centeredness movement, and is spiritually most healthy.

A clear example of the process is Jesus during the week before his death. There was a man who knew what was happening to him: he faced human death and consistently allowed others and God into his center of feeling and awareness. At the garden, struggling with decision making, he cared for the freedom of his disciples (Jn 18:9); on the cross he thought of a criminal who was his companion in death, prayed for his executioners, talked with his Father, entrusted his mother to John and John to his mother. As far as we can perceive, his consciousness and awareness of others showed a clear unselfishness. His center was not himself but rather others and the Father, his God. This gave him a great dignity and that unique greatness of being of the unselfish. He seemed clothed in that profound meaning and love which balance and order the tragedy and death which would foil peace and love for humankind. The overwhelming movements of destruction, anguish, despair, injustice, impotency, and failure seem to be absorbed by greater movements, much greater and powerful ones. The sacred movements of forgiveness, trust, abandonment to God's will, goodness, longing to be in paradise, care for his mother and disciples, and the like, take over, dissolve the destructive movements and make the image of that man what he is, a unifier, a new life, another light and vision for all of us who search.

The accounts of his life contain many other instances when we can see his lack of self-centeredness and selfishness. He avoided the crowd that would make him king; he thought of the possibility of being a star, the adored master of kingdoms, and he summarized once and for all: "You must worship the Lord your God, and serve him alone." (Mt 4:10; Lk 4:8.)

Remember how often he healed, and was aware of the afflictions and feelings of others. He was definitely not a selfish, self-centered man; this does not mean that he did not know who he was or where he was going.

Paradoxically, the self-centered person knows less who one is and what the meaning of one's life is, and has a much less clear sense of direction and mission. The reason is simple. Meaning, mission, and self-knowledge are generated by relation and relationships. I remember the case of a nineteen-year-old woman whom I asked in a group workshop: "Why are you here?" She said: "To know God." I questioned: "Why do you want to know God?" She replied: "That I might understand who I am."

Looking at God, Jesus knew better who he was. Looking at others he understood what his mission was. The wide open consciousness of the unselfish, unselfcentered individual allows meaning, mission, and expansiveness.

The Spirit of God, who was in Jesus and is in us, generates expansiveness and orientation. When we manage to unblock the Spirit, our lives take new movements and healthy transformation occurs.

The ultimate movement towards others driven by the Spirit of God in Jesus is the total self-giving which he perpetuated in the institution of a sacrament—a sign that means the sacred—called the Eucharist, a meal that means giving himself to be eaten and drunk. And he says: "He who eats my flesh and drinks my blood lives in me and I live in him." (Jn 6:56.)

Our ordinary daily lives require the constant symbolism and signification of our self-giving—or selfish self-taking. Gifts, phone calls, communication, and gestures between friends and lovers are signs and symbols of self-giving. Giving and taking, a flow of life and being. Their different degrees, equilibria, motivations and circumstances would determine whether the flow means love and comes from a holy spirit, or means selfishness and comes from neurosis or even a bad spirit. The movement of self-giving and unselfishness is more enjoyable and fulfilling than that of selfishness and self-centeredness.

When Jesus instructs his disciples on the proper stance to take towards others, he says: "anyone who wants to be great among you must be your servant." (Mt 20:27.) "If a man takes you to law and would have your tunic, let him have your cloak as well." (Mt 5:40.) "'Lord how often must I forgive my brother if he wrongs me? As often as seven times?' Jesus answered, 'Not seven, I tell you, but seventy-seven times'." (Mt 18:21–22.) "What I command you is to love one another." (Jn 15:17.) "If you wish to be perfect, go and sell what you own and give the money to the poor, and you will have treasure in heaven; then come, follow me." (Mt 19:21.) "For anyone who wants to save his life will lose it; but anyone who loses his life for my sake will find it." (Mt 16:25.)

The question is whether I can live in the sacred movements apparent in Jesus? The answer is that I can, we can. The Spirit of God is given to us. We can choose one direction or another.

The Movement of Self-Affirmation: Humility

I used to consider humility as self-effacement and self-denial; now I understand it as self-affirmation, and see it as an important movement of being. It is best to start with a parable. Once I was a gardener with a plot of land to care for. I remember my joy in seeing the flowers I had planted blossom. I had tulips, roses, and daisies. I watered them, weeded them, cultivated them, and trapped the animals that would have eaten them. I worked for months until they flourished. Then I took them to the chapel or my house or shared them with friends.

A gardener affirms the flowers and denies the weeds. A humble garden would be full of flowers and valued for what it is. A proud garden would be one that appears to be and is not. A garden that would choke the flowers would be a confused and self-destructive garden. *Garden* in itself means the affirmation of flowers.

Jesus affirms that he was the son and envoy of God. He did not affirm what he was not. That is humility: affirming who he was was in itself denial of what he was not.

Truthful self-affirmation is the essence of true humility. It has the beauty of a flower and the strength of a well-rooted tree. Affirmation of what one is not is ridiculous. It denotes emptiness, delusion, and untruthfulness. It is an evil, is sad, and generates useless weeds.

The movement of self-affirmation—knowing who I am in relation with my God and others—is a healthy movement of becoming. Who does God say that I am? Who does Jesus say that I am? He says that I am or can become one with him. God says that he is my Father, that I am his child, and that he loves me. Jesus says that as the Father sent him so he sends me. (*See* Jn 20:21.) If I love him, Jesus says, he himself, the Father, and the Spirit will live in me.

Have I the right to deny all that? I need to be humble to accept it. The affirmation of self is the affirmation of a deep relationship with the Father and Jesus. The real self in its depths is a relationship. The flowers are a relationship between the earth and the sun; without that, there would be no flowers.

My being is a relationship between mankind and God; without them I would not be. I belong to both. Jesus of Nazareth was and is the flowering of humanity. There is beauty in being; being what we are is the denial of what we are not.

The Movement of Peace

One kind of peace or order flows from outside in; another flows from some mysterious depths inside out.

"Peace I bequeath to you, my own peace I give you. . ." (Jn 14:27.) Jesus' gift of peace is the gift of ordering movement. The integration of God and man. The oneness. A new salvific, unifying movement of being, totally the opposite of sin and disorder. This he gave to his apostles.

Is that peace and power to order given to us? Where is it? Do we enjoy it? Do we live it and share it?

Part of it we live unconsciously; to a certain extent, we cannot escape the forces of God's presence and creation in us. Yet how beautiful and fruitful it would be to enter fully and consciously into that movement of peace and ordering, and to eliminate the obstacles of our sinfulness—resistance and movements opposed to the appeasing and integrating movement that Jesus gives us.

This movement is already given to us. How can we actualize and activate it? Could I some day say to others "My peace I give you," and give to them what Jesus gave me? Not that I would give peace fully, but that I would help to discover, share, enjoy, and develop it?

Could that be part of my mission in life? A sharing by grace in the mission of Jesus? I think it is; not only mine but of all of us who believe in our mystical connection with Jesus, who accept God in us and our being in him.

"My own peace I give you."

People who give peace are aware of and promote the movement of union between God and man. A movement that transforms individuals and mankind. People who give union and oneness from inside out, who understand and move within the mystical forces of a living, loving, creative, and present God.

Peace is a gift: a vision, a force, a life: indeed, God himself given to us to be given.

"My own peace I give you." That is, "my love, myself, and what was given to me I give to you." If this movement were unleashed, the universe would flourish into oneness, and the glory of the Father and Jesus would glow in creation.

The Movement of Coming Home

Coming home is a theme of the Parable of the Prodigal Son; perhaps in this movement lies the beauty of the parable as far as the figure of the younger son is concerned.

What would the directional movement of coming home mean to Jesus?

It is possible that he experienced in himself the feeling of homelessness. He was probably too young to recall exile in Egypt, but in his adult life he moved from one place to another. At one time he said that he was homeless. "Foxes have holes and the birds of the air have nests, but the Son of Man has nowhere to lay his head." (Mt 8:20.) Then he talked twice about the house of the Father—the temple (Jn 2:16-17) and heaven (Jn 14:2)—but especially of the home he and his Father would have in us: "If anyone loves me he will keep my word, and my Father will love him, and we shall come to him and make our home in him." (Jn 14:23.)

The movement of coming home is a centering movement, it is knowing where acceptance is, where love awaits, where forgiveness and mercy are unlimited. It is the knowledge of where peace and life are.

We all have our ideal of home. Houses or dwelling places are supposed to be homes, but often are not; perhaps they are incomplete images of home. Home is the place to rest, the climate to grow and become, a desired atmosphere of protection, security, warmth, understanding, and love. Most of us have temporary homes, more or less complete. God has prepared for us another home, the total home, and a place in it for us. "There are many rooms in my Father's house; if there were not, I should have told you. I am going now to prepare a place for you." (Jn 14:2.) "I want those you have given me to be with me where I am." (Jn 17:24.)

Jesus knew where he was going and undoubtedly had a sense of direction towards a complete, eternal home. Do I have it? Can I have it? Can you have it? Do we lose the ideal of home, the total, eternal home? Or are we too busy building houses, founding disappointments and frustrations, nesting in possessions of things and people, and worrying about properties?

Can I make my home in God, starting now? Can I lock into the movement towards the house of the Father where I will find unfailing love, the peace and joy of forgiveness, the welcome of a Father and the happiness of a family? Yes I can, we can.

The forces of transcending—not being satisfied with anything temporal or incomplete, the experience of exile, the partial human deaths, the searching for something more complete and total—reveal the love of God; all these draw us onward, help us to move towards home.

The Movement of Housing

> "One thing I ask of Yahweh
>   one thing I seek:
> to dwell in the house of Yahweh
> all the days of my life."
>   *(Psalm 27)*

We live in the house of the Lord, and we are the house of the Lord.

To walk towards the house of the Lord is to move under the protection and the warmth of God. He invites us repeatedly.

To this movement of ours towards the house of the Lord corresponds another movement, more admirable, and of even greater benefit to us. The Lord houses himself in us.

Our movement towards the house of the Lord could be motivated by many different reasons, such as insecurity, incompleteness, fear, and love. But God comes to dwell in us for only one reason: love.

I wish I could house myself in God and all that he means to me. Part of my desire should be to better allow him to dwell in me.

Housing is building; it prepares for a new homing, and recalls past homings.

Jesus housed his God, the Father, in himself; the Father eternally housed and homed Jesus.

I house and home the people I love in myself and it feels good to know that I am housed and homed in other people.

One thing I long for, to live in the house of the Lord all the days of my life. There where my God lives, with him, and in him.

The Movement of Bonding to the Order of God
   in Our Midst

God's order is more than God's presence. It is an active efficient presence, an involvement, and in a still deeper sense, a life.

God's life is the midst of us, in us individually and in the midst of us, giving us life, energy, being, and movement. In the midst of us, bonding, uniting, creating a family, a greater and more complete entity, gifting us with communication, communion, love, belonging, and the greater life of a social common being, the body of Christ. In the midst of us forming a new creation, the Christ-genesis that Teilhard de Chardin talked about.

My longing for order is endless. I long for an order in my activities and emotions which often eludes me. I long for social order around me. I love and admire nature's order when I see it. Beauty reminds me of inner and outer order. I feel secure in ordered social systems. Chaotic traffic unnerves me. These are simple examples. I am trying to express how deeply a sense and a longing for order is imbedded in me.

Moreover, there is spiritual order; it goes beyond traffic laws, social mores, personal feelings and emotions, and human activities. Spiritual order is deeper, all-encompassing, mystic. It is the ordering with God. This is an order—a law, a life, an active presence—which is given to us freely,which we can discover and activate if we would. For the order of God is in us and in our midst.

Jesus discovered and activated his order with God. So he called him Father. He discovered the order of sonship, the order of knowing. "Father. . . eternal life is this, to know you. . . ." (Jn 17:1–3.) The order of adoring: "You must worship the Lord your God. . . ." (Mt 4:10.) The order of serving: "the Son of Man came . . . to serve." (Mt 20:28.) The order of love: "love one another as I have loved you." (Jn 15:17.)

Jesus undoubtedly suffered disorders: the disorders of temptations, hunger, thirst, rejection, and the social evils of his time. He was misunderstood, accused, judged, and killed. Many of those disorders we too know and suffer. In spite of them, in the midst of them, and beyond them, Jesus found an order, one more powerful than disorder, one lasting and total, the order with the Father, his God.

The question is: can we also find that order, as a

source of life, security, happiness, and hope? Yes, indeed. It is in us and among us.

Does it mean that we will eliminate all the other disorders? Not necessarily. But it does mean that we will tolerate them differently and that we can be free from them. How different it is to go on a trip somewhere where nobody waits for you or where you know no one, than to go to a place where you love someone and someone loves you. Tolerating the confusion and pain of the travelling is quite different. We gladly suffer them when the power and the energy of human love is there.

Once at an airport I met a lady in her sixties who wanted to take a bus to another terminal. She carried an airplane ticket and a piece of paper which had an address written on it. She was from a foreign country and could not speak the language. The bus conductor was confused because he could not understand her. As I was the next in line, I offered to help. I asked the lady where she was going, she replied: "I'm going to see my daughter whom I have not seen for six years." She extended her arm and showed me the ticket and the address. I realized that she was continuing her trip on the flight I was taking. I offered to accompany her and I asked her where she was from, how long she had been traveling, whether she had flown before and how long it had been since she had eaten anything. She began or ended all her short answers with the refrain: "I want to see my daughter, I have not seen her for six years." I invited her to share a meal, and we called her daughter from the airport.

I cannot forget her. I saw how much she loved her daughter and what the power of love can do. She went to a foreign country—she did not know its language. She had never traveled in a plane. But she was not afraid of being lost, she was not aware of dangers. Her luggage was just one thing—a great love for her daughter and a longing to see her again.

The power of love is overwhelming. If you ask anybody to travel for days through unknown roads among strangers, to forget about eating or drinking, selfishness would always stand in the way, if one has no love to guide one. The power of love sets off mysterious movements in the person which overcome all difficulties.

Yes, the order of God is in us and among us. In God we live, move, and exist. Our God lives, moves, and exists in us. God's order, his law, is a movement because it is life. It is not like some orders or laws that we perceive as static, burdensome, and lifeless. It is a joyful movement and a great feeling, the movement of ordering and integrating which always generates peace and happiness. Discovering and sharing such ordering movement is a sacred task and it is like discovering an inexhaustible treasure. Blessed are those who let God's order move them for they shall become one with him.

The discovery that God's order is moving and drawing us gives a feeling of peace and life that no words can describe it. It is blissful. The order is in us and we are in it.

Part 2

Communicating with the Living God: Prayer as a Movement

A Commentary on the "Our Father"

One who finds the movements of prayer within is like one who discovers a spring or an artesian well, or inexhaustible underground wealth.

Inside each human being there are divine currents of life, powerful and refreshing. When we get in touch with them, we discover a little more who we are. Prayer can be a path in that discovery and a means to draw out the refreshing waters of being.

The divine movements within the human being result from God's presence and grace; they are a gift that comes with life, and are not easily destroyed. These movements are from the Holy Spirit.

The best survey of such life-giving movements is found in Jesus' prayer, the Our Father, which forms a summary of his attitudes and inner movements, and which he wanted to share with his followers. Perhaps those movements and forces explain his centeredness, his strength, his security, his peace and order, his depth, and the end result of his life, that amazing union and oneness with God, whom he called *Abba*—Father.

The divine movements within humankind and the individual human being are undeniable existential reality. Rather than trying to prove their existence, I would like to point them out and call to your attention their beauty and their power to make human life blossom.

"Our": *The Movement of Expansive Becoming One with Others*

Unification or oneness is an integrating movement, a harmonizing process. The human body, for example, as any living organism, is composed of many different parts with different positions and functions, yet is a unity. It operates as one, feels one, and grows with its uniqueness. There are many types and forms of oneness; humans associate and integrate into family units, into one language or another, one country or race, one block of ideology or beliefs.

Mysticism and Christianity, like other religions, discover and proclaim a oneness beyond genetic descent, common words, or decisions on political issues. This oneness overwhelms yet invigorates. The heart of mystical oneness, which we all come from the same source and evolve to the same point of being, is God. We belong to one another and all together belong to our God. There is a hidden unity among all human beings and the universe, which, when we manage to unearth it, will generate an exhilarating energy and light, will be an authentic revolution from within, and will give the world new horizons, new visions, new strengths, new order and peace.

Jesus was a focus of this movement of cosmic and mystical oneness in many directions. Oneness first with the Father, the generating and creative God, and consequently oneness with everyone that comes from God and goes to him.

The transition from the consciousness of myself as individual to the consciousness of us with another individual, and then to the us as the totality of mankind and the universe is part of that expansive movement of the becoming of the one.

This sounds like an abstract concept but it is a reality to be tasted and discovered. The linkage is already within. When selfishness begins to disappear, the human consciousness is ready to be flooded with the new consciousness of the total us, the one, the new body and soul of the total being. We are made to unite, integrate, harmonize, and assume a greater being. For that we have to let the forces and movements of unification influence and transform us. Not just at the level of consciousness but also at the other levels like feelings, perception, communication, imagination, and expectations.

Thus, Jesus proclaims and insists both that he is one with God but also that we are one with him, and in him with God. His last will could not be clearer: "Father, may they be one in us, as you are in me and I am in you." (Jn 17:21.) Becoming Christian means entering into the oneness that he discovered and to which he committed himself. Perhaps the real evolution of humankind is to see, feel, live, and share that total sense of oneness with God and others.

Our human differences would then matter little, because the power of oneness would invade and overcome all of them, like a great love overcomes and forgives little faults, or like the sunlight overpowers darkness and shadows.

God of unity and oneness, help us evolve into the one that we are, within which you gave us life. Open our eyes that we might see our oneness, help us feel the beauty and power of being one with you, in you, and with everybody.

Guide us well from the smallness of selfishness to the total openness of being in the eternal us with you and others. God, that evolving oneness will be the solution to our pains, insecurities, and stupid fights.

You have already made us one, and Jesus brought us that message and called us to live it; why cannot we see, feel, and share that basic depth of who we are?

I offer my life to you and all your people with whom I am one, to be a voice of that word, a prayer of that wish, an opening to that reality, a step further for the universe and humankind into the amazing movement of becoming one with you and everything that comes from you and goes to you.

Let me, let us, be able to say and believe with Jesus that we are one, and that this oneness is the only order and law which will liberate us from ourselves.

Amen.

"Father": The Movement of Coming From and Being Generated

All of us are sensitive to our roots, where we are from and whom we are from. In fact, a common formula on meeting is "I come from...; where do you come from?" These determine identity, expectations, and direction. We are also familiar with different levels of depths in such "coming from" both in time and geography. Where I came from originally is different from where I come from today or right now.

Jesus stated a new level of depth when he said "I came from the Father and have come into the world and now I leave the world to go to the the Father." (Jn 16:28.) That is an existential movement within him that he becomes aware of and charts his life by.

His "coming from" and "being generated" is a constant movement rather than an act. The movement starts in an act but becomes a constant flow. The energy flow in an electric lamp might start with a flick of a switch but needs a steady current. Life itself can be viewed as constant "coming from," "being generated" by God the Father.

I can truly say that I also come from God and go to God. That fact determines my identity, my direction, and my position in existence. True, I can choose to ignore or accept it. If I accept it, then the vision of my being here takes on new dimensions. Reading Jesus' life and the gospel narratives, we sense his deeply felt awareness of "coming from" and "being sent." Acknowledging that I am from God and go to God, I must face the question why I am here. Here lies the origin of a profound sense of mission: "I am sent." That movement is in all of us and every being that is.

When I say *Father* I thus proclaim a fact of being generated and a movement of coming from. Feelings associated with this particular movement are gratefulness, awe, respect, love, peacefulness, joy in existential order, and even the simple joy in just being. As proper movements of the Spirit of God, those feelings flow or flower from that first movement of coming from.

I also feel that I am responsible to my mission in being, humility and truth. When I say and feel the word *Father*, I dare to belong; it is like entering into space or mystical navigation with another set of coordinates, other gravity forces, and other energy sources. Why not travel with those movements which can in themselves build the meaning of my living? Why leave unused powers which we have all received freely and abundantly?

God, Father, constant origin of my being, help me discover the sacred movements which you put within me. When I have discovered them, help my enjoy riding in them towards you and life, and to share them with everybody.

"Who Art in Heaven": *The Movement of Being In*

Sometimes we consider being in as the end of movement: the journey is over, we have come to where we would be. But being there, being in, is not just being at the end of something, but much more. Being is an unending process; being in, being there is just the beginning of the total movement, of the perfect one. In this sense we can say that calm, quiet, peace, and harmony are the plentitude of movement.

Long ago we decided that where God is is not a place, although he is in every place, or rather all places are in him. Where God is, is in himself; that is heaven because that is plentitude, harmony, love, life, light—every attribute of the total, perfect being. Where God is there is movement, for within him there is the totality of movement; union or oneness, for he is love; totality of movement of life, for he is creator; totality of movement of compassion, for he forgives and redeems; totality of movement of expression and communication, for he reveals his love, his missions, himself.

"Father who art in heaven." That makes me think: "Where am I?" Where do I spend my existence: Am I in myself or outside of myself? in heaven or in hell? in order or in disorder? in peace, or in constant anxiety and insecurity? in things or in people? in the present, in the past, or rather in my dreams? Am I in reality or in delusions? Am I in God? Am I in heaven? Can I be?

Where was Jesus of Nazareth? He was in Palestine and Galilee. He was with his friends and disciples. He was with suffering people, the poor, the sick, and the sinners. He was in the synagogue, on the road, and in the temple; but cannot we say that he came to be in the Father, that his deeper being was really in the Father, his God? From there he was everywhere that his human being could reach. He immersed himself in God, was in

the Father as the Father was in him. He knew where the
Father was. He knew that he was going to the Father. And
he says to the apostles: "I am going now to prepare a place
for you... I shall return to take you with me; so that where
I am, you may be too." (Jn 14:2-3.) "Trust me, I have con-
quered the world." (Jn 16:33.) He began to be in heaven,
in God, before he came to us, and in this coming, paradoxically he never left, being one with the Father, he was
God, and he says:

> I will come back to you,
> In a short time the world will no longer see me;
> but you will see me,
> because I live and you will live.
> On that day
> you will understand that I am in my Father
> and you in me and I in you.
> Anybody who receives my commandments and
> keeps them will be one who loves me. . . .
> *(Jn 14:18.)*

"Cut off from me you can do nothing." (Jn 15:5.)

The application seems clear. Where should I be? In
Christ. He in me and I in him, as he was in the Father
and the Father was in him. Is that possible? It has to be.
Not only possible, but even easy, taking the proper path
and means. The heart of the matter is that we are already
in him and he is in us, because without him and outside
of God, nothing and nobody exists. So, if I am already
in God and God is in me, perhaps it is a question of not
blocking out that reality. Perhaps I do not see it because
I have my eyes closed and my heart locked, and my ears
plugged. Where am I? Just in worries, in my fears, in my
not-being? Can I move towards being, towards being in
heaven, that is, in peace, love, fulfillment, adoration, one
with my God, being in him?

> Father, who are in heaven, help me under-
> stand where I am and where I should be. Help me

be in you and to acknowledge and embrace the fact
that you are in me, so that I can begin in this life
to be in heaven, that is, in you.
            Amen.

If I can resolve my inner where, I have a place to be.
It will be of most importance to my being to decide where
I want to live, where I want to put my hopes, my dreams,
my stock, my future, my eternal life. I hear of people who
work all their lives to buy a house and spend most of their
income on it. I suppose that I can invest most of myself
in this other existential home, which has the advantage
of being the dream home of the future and, according to
the gospel, has been prepared for me. I shall make my
home in God, who is love, compassion, goodness, light,
security, and good company.

Near Jacob's well, a Samaritan woman once recognized Jesus as a prophet, and said "Our fathers wor-
shiped on this mountain, while you say that Jerusalem
is the place where one ought to worship." (Jn 4:21.) Jesus
answered that "the hour will come. . . when true worship-
ers will worship the Father in spirit and truth. . . ." (Jn
4:23.) There is that place in all of us, beyond geography
and space, where we can find the living God, that is,
spirit and truth, respect and adoration, union and love,
forgiveness and compassion, peace and silence, prayer
and humility. We can live in that inner place, where God
lives; that is where true evolution and growth takes the
human being to, that is where holy and wise people live.

With joy and excitement one can dedicate oneself
to building such a home. One can invite friends to visit
it, landscape it with the unique spiritual gifts. This, in
fact, can be the dream home of the future equipped with
spiritual energy, God's home in us and our home in God.

"Hallowed Be Thy Name": *The Movement of Setting
    Apart as Sacred*

"Hallowed" means "set apart as holy" or "consecrated"; this is the movement of recognizing the holy and the sacred, the movement of entering into the mystery of being. It is the movement of penetrating into the mysterious and mystical essence of life. It is the joyful movement of uniting the visible and the invisible, of allowing the mystical invisible to express itself through the visible. It is a rejuvenating movement of making life and existence holy, sacred, meaningful, connected and transcending.

> "Father, hallowed be thy name." Open my heart to recognize the holy, to adore, to never lose the sense of the sacredness of your presence. To recognize always the immense dimension of the holiness of your being and your presence impregnating our lives and making us sacred. Father, help me see that if I welcome your presence, it makes me and all of us sacred and holy, that you wanted to set us apart as your people and your children and that setting us apart makes us special, yours, sacred, holy. Father, help us see and enjoy the fact that we are your holy people. "Hallowed be thy name." Let me hear and speak your name with all the reverence and sacredness that I would be capable of, let me enter into the climate of holiness and sacredness. Help me avoid the temptation of secularizing, profaning, and ignoring the meaning of my being in you.

The movement of being set apart as holy and sacred, the movement of adoration, the movement of being a child of God and entering into the sacred oneness with the divine is a movement of joy. It is the salvific movement of redemption. It is the only movement that makes total sense within human existence. It is not difficult to understand the pain and destruction of the opposite movement: the unintelligent movement of denying or ignoring sacredness, holiness, God's presence, and the divine direction of life. This opposite movement would make us worthless and hopeless. It desecrates existence.

> Father, hallowed be thy name in the midst of us; help us live in the great joy of reverencing you within our lives and all around ourselves. Help us live in the sacred atmosphere of life and respect which is the only one in which a human being can breathe, grow, and become. Make that movement, hallowed be thy name, the deep and consistent cry of my life. Let other people, when they see me, recognize the sacredness of your presence and reverence you in me as we recognize you in Jesus. Let me see you in others in all your people who are set apart, made holy and sacred by your graces and your merciful love. Father, hallowed be thy name.

"Thy Kingdom Come": The Movement of Accepting God's Order and Kingdom

The term translated as the *kingdom of God* in the gospels generally means the *reign of God*, his being king and being welcomed as king. I used to think that God's order and presence was supposed to come from above. Lately I realized that it comes from within. The distinction is relevant because it guides my expectations. An image that helps me to realize its coming from within is the growing of flowers. They do not come down from above, but they come from within out. Life in general seems to do so.

Wishing for God's order is a movement which prepares for it, it is a stance of expectation and hope; it is the flexibility of giving oneself to that order, entering into it and letting it order and harmonize oneself.

God's order, reign, and kingdom are already in us, like a law imprinted in the depths of our being. Do you see the law of gravity which is inside all physical objects or beings within the realm of the earth or other planets? Still deeper within living human beings is the law of love and order, the aspiration to higher existence and peace. Yet we have to activate it, to wake up to it, to proclaim it, and to let ourselves live its gentle and powerful dynamics.

"Your kingdom come," can be interpreted as your love come, your compassion, your liberating power, your mercifulness, your light and gifts, your presence, your word, your voice.

> May you come to us, God you yourself, and be in us as you always wanted: that will be enough to divinize our living and to clarify our existence.
> This movement of expectation and hope opens me to receive life eternal and unlimited; it can be a constant of my spirit. It will make a difference in my life, the difference between a person with immeasurable hope and one lost in futility and despair. Come, God, come from within, into me and into us; we are your people and belong to you. Without you we become very confused and empty; in you is our order and meaning. Come, and stay, as you did in Jesus and all your holy ones.

Smaller, partial movements should be integrated into greater, more total movements. The movements of driving an automobile—shifting gears, turning curves, pulling out into the passing lane—are coordinated and integrated into a greater total movement of direction and good.

In Jesus the human movements of relating to himself, the disciples, the people, and even enemies were coordinated and integrated into a greater, total movement towards the Father.

Such integration is better when we are aware of it, when we intend and properly direct it.

Yet since some forces are given and the greater movements are gifts which originate in God, we must also passively let them interact and happen. Here the prayer of acceptance and the due active abandonment into God's creation is valuable; they let his action operate in us, let oneself, with faithfulness and trust, be driven or piloted by the God Spirit.

"Thy Will be Done": *The Movement of Harmony and Coordination of Wills*

Jesus achieved total harmony with the will of God, sometimes painfully, other times joyfully. His total harmony ended in the achievement of oneness with the Father. He would say my will is the Father's will and I want nothing else. It implied the elimination of conflict between his own desires and the Father's. Ultimately, it was a movement of unification and integration, the supreme inner integration of a human being.

How do I distinguish my will, wants, desires, and intentions, from God's? How do I know whether I am in the right path or not? How do I integrate my being into God's will? Do I want to? We may fear the uncertainty of these situations. Everything seems enveloped in fog; yet there are clear markers and guideposts.

Imagine that you are traveling to your favorite city. If I ask you, "How do you know what road you are on? If the curves point the road sometimes east, other times west, how do you know if eventually it is taking you there? How do you know whether you are moving or not and at what speeds?" Your answer would be: "I know."

Do we know when we are good or bad? Yes, we do. Do we know when we are getting closer to God? Yes, we do. Do we know when we move spiritually? Of course we know. At times, the road twists east or west; but we know where we are heading to. And, as we travel, we have maps, signs, odometers, weather service and travelers' advice.

Did Jesus use means similar, though spiritual? I believe so. There are "signs and wonders", big and small on the road. They need not be supernatural, startling events. Feelings and hunches are signs; other travelers, with their information and advice about road traps and good or bad weather conditions are signs. Jesus searched, listened to John the Baptist, prayed, struggled. He was tempted to go in the wrong direction. But he did not.

"Your will be done." A movement of harmony with God, with the God who is already inside. We have an inner compass, if we know how to read it. How do I know when I am selfish and when I serve others or God? Easy. It is easy to know where I want to go and how.

How do I hear music? I listen. The will of God is always sounding within and without. What changes is our listening. We have to listen. Maps, books, advice, events: though all these will help, the road is the road. The will of God is already inside us and somehow is us, is me, is an inner movement, a sacred part of my existence. The will of God is union and oneness with him and the universe—that is what love means.

Imagine for an instant that every human being would harmonize, would accept and obey that movement of union and oneness within, with all others, and with God; can you picture the order, light, power, and universal joy that it would generate? Is it possible? Yes, it is; at least, I can make it possible for me.

Let each one be responsible for his or her part. "Your will be done." No wonder that was a directional movement and attitude in Jesus. It can be ours too; it is worthwhile to spend one's life living this attitude, moving in this direction.

"Give Us This Day Our Daily Bread": *The Movement of Trust*

Trust has its roots in security. The movement of

trust implies, like most psychological movements, a vision, a direction and a consequent feeling. But trust is more than a feeling.

I like to see Jesus trusting in his Father, relying on him, expecting, experiencing security, abandoning himself in his "Abba," Father. His trusting embodies a vision of a provident God, a God of an active and efficient love.

Jesus experiences the security of a God that makes him, guides, sends, cooperates and calls him deeply and consistently. A faithful God, the God of his ancestors, a God who is always there, a God who generated the trust which is security with a feeling of love and union.

In relating to individuals or groups, we know whom we can trust and whom we would rather not. Trust comes from union, for it is a well-grounded hope.

Naturally we also know the good feelings of trust. It always carries with it peace; it is a good ground to grow love; it is related to believing someone. We have experienced as well distrust and its feelings, the numerous fears that distrust brings with it, underlying judgments, rejections, isolation, and pain.

Knowing God makes trust in him increase. In the prophets and Jesus, that trust relationship with their God is easily identifiable and quite beautiful to observe. Relating properly to God inevitably creates in the human being movements of security, confidence, peace, and well-being. "The Lord is my shepherd, there is nothing I shall want." (Ps 23.)

In my bones, and I assume in every Christian, there is a law of trust. Given the choice, we prefer to live in trust rather than distrust. To a certain extent, we can recognize a similar movement in pets. We can observe the trust of a dog in its owner, and with it comes joy and faithfulness.

I want to trust in my God, like a wounded sheep would trust a good shepherd. God, it is good to trust in you

Forgiveness and other signs of love increase the trust. It seems necessary that sound spiritual life develop into boundless trust. There is a presentiment that this movement of trust is the prelude of great blessings.

For many years in religious life, I have desired and searched for a clearer relationship with my God. I do not recall the same impulse I now feel to trust my God. It is a movement that comes with a quiet joy and peace. The image of Jesus who in trust throws himself into the Father, even during his crucifixion, comes to my mind often and enlightens my path.

This movement goes directly to the essence and the heart of my God, the thrust is a self-giving, at the core level of my being beyond actions, word, and circumstances, a self-giving which is love and which produces at new depths in me that quiet, ineffable well-being and peace mentioned above.

All the endeavors of my past life are well worthwhile if they take me to the mere threshold of new state of trust and peaceful joy.

I sense the gentle presence of a loving God who cares about me and guides me. He is my horizon and my security, I am his servant and his son. He is with me, he takes care of me.

My desire in life is to serve and love my God. He has guided me towards himself and liberated me from many traps, from myself and many other structural traps which humans build to protect ourselves from our insecurities.

Apparently I have been detached and separated from many securities and stand alone and structurally naked in the world, but paradoxically I feel secure in the palm of God's hands, and I feel his gentle warmth; having nothing I have everything. Being humanly uprooted, I am given the security and rootedness in my God. Feeling totally deprived and poor, I stand in the wealth and richness of my God with the strong soothing feeling of the psalm: "The Lord is my shepherd, there is nothing I shall want." (Ps 23.)

I do not deserve such great blessing, but let it be for the glory of my God.

The impulse or movement to trust comes with a great new sense of poverty—inner freedom from everything and only attachment or union with my God; with a feeling of sacredness that establishes a relationship with everything and everybody in the sacredness, so that even if the freedom of poverty detached me from everything and everybody, the sacredness and respect would unite me with everybody and everything. And then, there is the trust movement, another sense of peace and order so delicate that it is hard to explain. It is like someone orders me from inside out and makes me obedient and submissive to an order which I know is God's presence.

This order of peace is sacred. I believe it was always there, and that all could draw from it like the deep waters of a sacred well. But a process of grace, liberation, consecration, and submission must bring one to those waters of new life. We cannot reach them by our own effort, for the process itself is a gift. Our God enjoys guiding us towards it, towards himself.

I feel consolation being in the Society of Jesus, forming part of the companions of Jesus. An unexplainable grace. Consolation in being poor through freedom, consecrated through living in a sacred dimension, and peaceful through obedience to the impulses of my God.

I see a movement of trust throughout the life of Jesus; I feel such a movement in myself as a new, unexpected gift. This movement is a unifying gift; it not only leads me to trust my God, but it overflows into trusting people and life, friends and enemies, no matter what their motivation might be. It is a mysterious, mystical movement through ineffable joy.

Thank you God, Father, Friend. Into your hands I commend my being with all its relationships and dimensions.

The movement of trust eliminates fears. We have existential fears, fears of not being, insecurities and questions about who we are, about the future and stability of our being, our continuation. Corresponding to such fears and insecurities, God gives a security and trust which heals our anxieties, and fills our being with mysterious, powerful peace.

The movement of trust is a sacred movement, inspired by the Spirit of God, which consecrates my life. Trusting, I give my being to my God. I am like a child who throws himself into the arms of father or mother, and in so doing loves and is loved. Thus when I trust and throw myself into the arms of my God, I accept his love and security, I give him the joy of protecting me, and I feel raised up into him. Trusting is truly uplifting.

When I entrust my whole inner being to my God, I entrust him as well the peripheral dimensions of existing, such as physical health and material and emotional needs.

No matter how much we would deny it, we all need trust at many levels. The movement of trust means not complacency, but its contrary. Trust generates cooperation; self-giving enhances creativity and work. One gives all one has, and receives a new underlying feeling. It is the difference between doing something alone or doing it with another; walking in fear and insecurity or with security, confidence, and existential insurance.

Good, healthy religion develops a relationship with a living God that necessarily leads into trust, that beautiful embrace from inside with a powerful and gentle God. Trust becomes a mystical state of being. It is perceptible in Jesus and our saints, yet all of us seem to be created for this state.

"Forgive Us Our Trespasses as We Forgive Those Who Trespass against Us": *The Movement of Forgiveness*

The movement or attitude of forgiveness comes from love. Forgiveness manifests the power of activated love. It is a clear sign that realized union is more powerful than separation. Like any real movement of love, it is joyful and constructive. Like most human beings, I have often faced two choices. I was injured, in fact or in fancy; the choice of revenge or forgiveness confronted me. Retaliation attracted by a vision of concrete justice, self-protection, victory, and dominance. The other choice, forgiveness, was in a sense less seductive, for it could seem to be weakness, cowardice, impotence, stupidity and folly.

However, the free exercise of this second choice can be an act not of weakness, but of inner strength, not of cowardice but of a brave and powerful spirit, not a retreat in confused impotence but rather an advance with greater power. It requires a greater power to forgive than to punish. Only the person who is secure enough that he does not feel threatened by an offense can joyfully exercise the power of forgiveness. Above all, revenge and punishment can mean insecurity and fear, a sign of smallness of being rather than greatness.

One who has everything can afford to give up something. For the one to whom something is everything, losing that thing is losing everything. Yet further: for one to whom having is being, to lose what he has is to lose being. For the person to whom having is secondary, losing what he has is affirming his being. This sounds like a riddle; perhaps it is the riddle of life which we are all share. Jesus said save—own—your life and you will lose it, give it and you will have it. (*See* Mt 10:39; Mt 16:25; Mk 8:35; Lk 9:24.) It is a paradox and the explanation of being as well.

If I could give away much money, or even let others take as much as they wanted, without much changing my bank balance, I would be very wealthy. If I could risk my reputation, status, and intellectual or affective human properties—or even let others take them for their own reasons and intentions—and did not feel threatened, diminished or destroyed, and took no defensive or vengeful measures; if, that is, I still forgave, still loved, I would consider myself wealthy in being and in love. Then I would consider myself Christian, Christlike, a living continuation of Christ.

Is that possible? Not on my own power, but yes, with the virtue and power of my God which he gives us freely and abundantly.

Perhaps I am lucky and blessed when someone offends me, attacks or tries to destroy me, because then I have the golden opportunity of showing the strength and the presence of my God in my life. Another dimension can grow in me at that time: the dimension of forgiveness and love, of the presence of my God. Many would not understand this, but that is their concern.

The security and peacefulness of one who has grown enough in union with his God to forgive, to love those who harm him, are joyful and great beyond comparison.

"And Lead Us Not into Temptation But Deliver Us from Evil": *The Movement of Freedom*

Religion provides a unique and special freedom quite unlike any other. There are many kinds of freedom; the two basic kinds are freedom to and freedom from. For example, money frees you from many inconveniences to do things or to get things. In some societies one enjoys freedom of speech, of education, of choice, of work, of vote, and so forth.

But religion offers freedom from evil, freedom from death everlasting, and the subtle, valuable freedom from oneself; again, it offers the spiritual freedom to be and become: it frees new and divine powers or forces within the person which result in a superior and supernatural life.

Freedom from evil is very important. We cannot enumerate here all the types of evil that exist and affect us, but we will mention a few. Some evil comes from within me: evil thoughts, desires, selfishness. Somehow, such evil movements, often unforeseen, spring from within to poison my life. We all know them although we cannot explain many of them. Here the Christian religion, I found, is a great medicine and liberating power. For example, generosity and self-giving free me from selfishness. Humility, or acceptance and adoration of God, frees me from the stupidity of pride and provides wisdom. Chosen detachment from things and people frees me from the slavery of being possessed either by things or people, and of possessing things or people. A kind of chosen poverty deeply liberates the person. Likewise, we can be possessed by ideas or even proud in the possession of ideas. That is why St. John of the Cross joined knowledge and possessiveness:

> In order to arrive at having pleasure in everything,
>   Desire to have pleasure in nothing.
> In order to arrive at possessing everything,
>   Desire to possess nothing.
> In order to arrive at knowing everything,
>   Desire to know nothing. . . .
> Such freedom give an unexplainable joy.

Religion frees within me forces which I did not know I had: the power and force to be merciful, compassionate, to believe, to hope, to love or unite through the spiritual love of being. This last differs from uniting through things, actions, ideas, emotions, and objectives. These latter unions or loves come mostly from temporal happenstance, but the union or love that comes through the spirit, though it might include temporal ones, is everlasting, much greater, purer and naturally more enjoyable.

For many years I did not understand spiritual love and union; I would get it confused with all the others. But now I am beginning to grasp it, and am willing to spend the time waiting and searching for it. Usually, other people or circumstances can destroy temporal loves and unions, but the one I am talking about is practically indestructible. To unite and love in a way that cannot be lost or destroyed is a great and secure joy; it liberates from fears and temporality.

Christianity frees me also from outside evils, and enables me to transcend them. Forgiveness liberates me from hatred and revenge and heals many wounds. Sharing and giving liberates me from the greed and selfishness of others. Faith frees me from despair, confusion, and contradictions.

Just when we let God enter our lives, a liberating and saving process begins to free us from all human boundaries and raises us up to the divine freedom of being. This process takes its human time; it must be experienced rather than discussed or argued.

Peace frees me from disorder. God liberates me from myself, and gives me the real me, makes me more human. For a human being is more complete when blended with divinity. And this great joy is waiting for all.

Religion of course offers the ultimate liberation from all the limitations and cages of this world into a totally new existence in time. Many would frown on this idea. They would condemn it and say that a liberation which disengages me from the world is either a cop-out or just idealism. But let me explain. The liberation I am talking about does not separate me from the world or life; quite the contrary: it unleashes creativity and involvement, and adds to them the element of freedom.

One can go to work in the fields as a prisoner in a concentration camp. Or just because one enjoys growing flowers and freely choose to do so. Society, needs, greed, questionable responsibilities, or network obligations can trap one and force one to make the best of things. But religion frees me to be involved with the world in a free, creative, joyful way. I would not trust a religion which forces me into the field, and does not liberate the very being of a person with the element of joy.

Part 3

Becoming One with the Living God

Introduction

Power of any kind is fascinating. Look at economic power and the impotency of the economically poor, political or social power, or even the hysterical power to command attention. We associate being with power and nonbeing with powerlessness. Perhaps we all crave for some kind of power; existentially, I would say, we crave for being. Being important means having some form of power.

The spiritual world also contains powers, of quite a different kind. Of course, people that dedicate themselves to spiritual realities often become entangled by any type of human powers. But the spiritual realm contains quite different kinds of powers.

Jesus of Nazareth refused the offer of political and social powers, yet he exercised and gave to his disciples unique, amazing powers of another order. For example, he once said to a paralyzed man "your sins are forgiven." (Mt 9:2; Mk 2:5; Lk 5:20.) Questioned immediately about his power to forgive, he cured the man physically. He exercised the powers of a God; of those powers, he emphasized that the power to believe and the power of loving surpass the power to change a physical law. Those who believe in him can become children of God (Jn 1:12.) A human being can love God and make himself the dwelling place of God. (Jn 14:23.) The power to live in him conquers death: "whoever lives and believes in me shall never die" (Jn 11:26.)

Christianity gives the human being divine powers. I am not inventing them; they are realities that Jesus of Nazareth discovered and passed on to us. If we accept them, it is easy to picture a new age of religion and transformation of mankind. Let us not fall into the infantile delusion that the chief divine power is the ability to astonish everybody with extraordinary miracles. The powers I am talking about are greater and more normal. A God does not need to impress.

There are the powers of being and becoming. There are the powers of growth and responding, the inner power of freedom and liberation, for religion is a liberating process. There is the power of a divine identity: sonship, a relationship with God by which one becomes an heir, a son or daughter. The misunderstood power to forgive makes a human being overcome all the destructive powers that we use on one another individually or socially. The astonishing powers in Christianity of belonging, unification, sharing, and communicating would revolutionize humankind in humanly unforeseeable ways, if fully realized.

I can only begin to talk about them poorly, and hope that the process of activation take place in us. I can picture people who would pass through life pointing out gifts and powers, discovering them or uncovering them, and giving them away to those to whom they belong.

Jesus made the crippled walk, the blind see, the deaf hear, the bound free, the dead live, and he told his disciples to do the same. However, greater powers than those of physical liberation are those of moral or spiritual liberation. I can see Jesus say: Go and tell those who think that they are just temporal human beings that they can be—if they want—eternal children of God, one with God, sharers of divinity. Is not that a kind of liberation for and from mankind?

Go and tell those who think they are nothing that they are the body of Christ, sent as angels and messiahs, messengers and anointed children of God. Is this not a liberation from nothingness and indignity?

Go and announce to those bound by sin and evil that their sins are forgiven, that they can be free from evil and themselves. Is this not even better than seeing or hearing? Go and tell the lonely and rejected that God wants to be one with them, regardless of their education, job, race, or status.

This doctrine of the gift of powers, if taken seriously, may seem extravagant; yet it is the gospel of Jesus, it is his good news. Why should we demean it? And with what right?

I can picture an institution that would promote people's spiritual powers, giving them to the individuals instead of restricting them, somehow by activating in the individual those God-given great human powers, it would liberate new forces in mankind. Such an institution would liberate rather than bind.

The very term *institution* sounds binding. True, institutions are necessary and good. Yet we need a movement of unleashing, unbinding, liberating, activating and actualizing the forces and potentials inside us—gifts which we have no right to stifle or diminish in any way.

I can see the church giving powers to people, in the name of the Father and of the Son and of the Holy Spirit.

Sacramental Powers

Writing about sacramental powers does not diminish the value or importance of the sacramental acts or rites; quite the contrary. Yet we must keep in mind the important distinctions between act and process, between act and actualization. The act actualizes. What is actualized is usually greater than the act. For example, the act of switching on the light actualizes the electrical lighting of energy and power.

The sacraments signify and actualize what we are. What we are is greater than the sign with which we actualize and signify it. For example, the sacramental ceremony of baptism or matrimony might last only half an hour; they signify and actualize a reality not limited to half an hour. Sacramental acts signify and actualize forces and gifts from God in us; properly unleashed, these gifts create a divine dynamism within the human being. Such dynamics transform the human being into a new creation, a new being somehow, with new horizons, new identity, new forces, and new reason to be.

Baptism

Baptism signifies the power to become an heir of God, to enter God's family, to achieve a new great identity by accepting divine life within ourselves. Let me begin with a parable. Most of us have credit cards and membership cards. They give us credit power or an identification power. It is enough to show a club membership card in good standing to be accepted and to enjoy all the privileges of the club. Imagine a membership that would ensure your entrance and rights of heaven, God's club. Moreover, imagine adoption papers stating that one really became God's son or daughter.

The value of a membership card is not the card itself but what it signifies and represents. Another image is that of a lottery. Can you imagine what it would be like to win a lottery whose prize is ten thousand dollars a month for life? It is true that we must keep a card in good standing, and turn in a valid lottery ticket.

And so it is with a sacrament. The reality of baptism is greater and more beautiful than these images. The value of baptism is not just the act or the rite, but what they signify and entitle one to. Baptism goes beyond the ritual to a new identity, to the privilege of calling God Father, to belonging to the order of the divine; baptism gives us the family powers of security, love, bonding, joy, and freedom from death and human condition. Through baptism we receive the power to celebrate, share, enjoy and proclaim who we are.

It is a gift, we just have to accept it. Sometimes our selfishness impairs our ability to accept gifts. The power that we have to accept the free gift from God of being his children is to open ourselves to feel totally wanted and loved. The gift of divine sonship transcends this life and retirement into eternal life.

How enjoyable it is to feel accepted and wanted by someone, unconditionally without fears. Because of my sensitivity and my circumstances of comings and goings and spending most of my life in foreign lands, I am keenly aware of being accepted or rejected; I know how it feels. Who does not, to some degree or another?

Jesus knew and felt his own sonship. He then pointed to us and said that, if we wanted, we could have it and enjoy it as he did. "Father," he said, "that the world might know that you have loved them as you love me" (Jn 17:23, variant.) He also told us to go and baptize. That means, go and give what you have to others, tell them that they too can have it, that it is freely given, that sonship is for all of us. That it is a treasure to be discovered and enjoyed. Go and proclaim who you are, children of a God, and they are too if they so choose. Go and celebrate, share, who you are, rejoice in your new identity.

Do you see what this entails? Here is another power: we can baptize. We can help others discover who they are and celebrate and share it. This can be a life process, not just a once in a lifetime act. To those who do not know who they are we can reveal their identity. We can open up life to those who have no hope. Those with no sense of belonging we can bring into a real family.

This is a power to save. We have it. It bothers me that we sometimes forget who we are and what we have, and that consequently we do not exercise and enjoy our identity and power. The mere awareness and practice of this power to baptize is more than enough to make a person totally happy and his or her life completely meaningful.

The power to receive, celebrate, proclaim, and share our identity and sonship rights is given to all of us, to those who accept them. All of God's children should know what they are given by the Father and taught to enjoy it.

Confirmation

"Who do men say that the Son of Man is? ... But who do you say that I am?" (Mt 16:13, 15.)

Was Jesus looking for confirmation? Support? Did he need others to believe in him? Was he human? I believe that like all of us he needed confirmation and support in his human process of growth. Simon Peter gave it to him, John the Baptist gave it to him, his mother believed in him, Mary and Martha loved him.

Is there a unique power that we have, not just at the human level of believing in one another, but also at a deeper spiritual level, to confirm, to support, to help others become and grow? I am sure there is.

Many times I have seen in myself and in others the effect of being believed and trusted. It is like having some fuel to be and an engine to help keep us going. It awakens new energies, hope, and desire to be in a person. The Christian is a life-giving person who believes in himself and others not just in relation to human endeavors but also in relation to the divine dimension of our being, our sonship.

We likewise have the power to discourage, doubt others, create distrust, be sarcastic and destructive. Do we confirm one another in what we are before God and the world? How much do we use that power to confirm and affirm? Do I go through life believing or doubting, affirming or discouraging?

Should the ability and power to confirm be reduced to a once-in-a-lifetime ceremony or does that sacrament signify forces in us that we can use consistently through life? If we weighed in the balance our use of the power of affirmation against denial, confirmation and belief against discouragement and distrust, how would it look?

I see Jesus being affirmed and believed by some, disbelieved and mistrusted by many. But he affirmed others, he believed in us, he trusted sinners, he proclaimed the kingdom for all; he gave life. Can we do the same? He wants us to and we can.

Liturgy of the Word

Jesus is the human manifestation of God. St. John calls him the Word (Jn 1:1). He is a message and a messenger at the same time. A word and a message of life, hope, union, reconciliation, and freedom.

There are written messages and living ones. Often written ones mean the living ones. It is nice to receive a letter from a friend but it is better to receive the friend.

Could my life and your life be a sacred living message, a sacred word? Can it be a manifestation of God and Christ living in you and in me? In fact that is what should be for a Christian. It can be. It is.

Could life then be like a liturgy of the living word where by we would express and listen to the sacredness of our being? Would not that be beautiful? "Too idealistic," some would say. Not really, because we are sacred. When I see and react to the sacredness of myself and others, I express it, relate to it, receive it and proclaim it.

When I look and listen to creation from a mystical dimension, I glorify my God and the meaning of my life. When we treat a little child with respect and wonder, we recognize and express the mystery of sacredness in him or her, the connection with God. When instead of brooding on my bad evil feelings I move to my good and holy feelings—God-like or God-powered—and I relate with them to myself, others, and the world, I communicate sacredness, beauty, the presence of God. Then I am another message, another word, another music, another liturgy.

Can we live in a symphony of sacredness, mysticism, goodness and awareness of God? We can and we do. It is certainly more rewarding and pleasant than the opposites to Christianity. It is the sacred symphony of living messages that God is with us and in us. If we would undertake the task of expressing and sharing the God in us, even if only a few started to do it fully, the music would be heard at the ends of the earth and at the end of time. A new celebration would overtake mankind.

The Power to Reconcile

Christianity actualizes this amazing power of people to reconcile in an especially beautiful way. It amazes me and somehow awes me. I have experienced myself moved to the depths of my bones by anger, bitterness, disillusionment, and perhaps hatred, authentically divisive powers. Christianity and the Spirit of my God have always called me back to peace, reconciliation, forgiveness and love. Then I experienced myself in quite a different light.

Put it this way: if I enacted and practiced the full capacity that the Spirit of my God gives me to unite, reconcile, forgive, and love, I would make such a dent in the world that it would shake its structure. I am not talking grandiosely; it is not a matter of my being important or not. What I am talking about is an awesome power that you and I have, all of us who would accept the grace of Christianity. The sacrament properly signifies a sacred and sacramental power that would change people and the world from separation to union, from loneliness to oneness, from distrust to security and peace, from emptiness to fulfillment, were it only set free within us.

The power to reconcile is the power and movement to love, it is one of the most beautiful, practical and effective powers of Christianity. It unites me with God, with myself, and with the universe.

Let me talk more in the concrete. I know what hate and disunion are. I have suffered them. They lead me nowhere, they are tornados that destroy whatever they touch in me. They make me terribly self-centered and they become a most unproductive energy. They build defensiveness, pride, trickery and ugly pettiness. If I can live clean of hate, why should I not?

Let us turn over the coin. I have also lived, and I want to live, in another movement, one of reconciliation. I have never felt better than when I could conquer my bad feelings, or rise above them, and, in the Spirit of my God, keep loving, forgiving, uniting, being open to life—even if some hurt remained. The peace, the light, the cleanness inside, the joy, the greatness, the harmony are good, feel good. And I know that I am not talking about just feelings, although they say a lot. But still more important is the reconciling movement itself. It is from God, it is the greatness of God and his justice. It is a movement that leads directly into God.

Reconciling and reuniting are greater than the power of dividing and destroying. Can you see life? It is all a force of unification. Can you imagine all the parts fitting into the meaningful whole? Imagine that the whole is the entire cosmos and—beyond the cosmos— the intrinsic total wholeness beyond time and physics of being with God. It is already here, it is in us. It is love. I am talking about a love that is different than desires, or likings or needs, or attachments, or sexuality; it is the love that forgives, that respects, that gives without taking, that believes beyond disillusionment, that hopes into eternity beyond our time.

We can do it, we can unify with a sacred love vertically, horizontally and in all directions, totally. I wish I could communicate clearly what I see.

Jesus had the power to reconcile man with God and with the very essence of being, and he gave it to us. It is a vision, a hope, a sacred movement, a oneness. It is real. We have it. The sacrament of reconciliation is the power to forgive and receive forgiveness, that is love.

I have forgiven many times, both in the name of the church, of my God and of myself. It gives others peace, acceptance, joy, well-being, security, strength and new life. If we can give those, why not give them constantly and fully. Why not? It feels quite good, and it is beautiful. Besides, his commandment was "love one another." (Jn 13:34.) Forgiveness has great power. Why not open my being and give it totally? I would gain much. I would gain the universe and that is little; I would gain God. I would actualize a divine power given to me in grace by the God that lives in me and loves me.

Can anybody do that? Of course. How? Do not we

learn more difficult tasks in life? Do not we learn to actualize our skills to utter sounds and understand signs, to use the power of our hands and feet, to put in and take out money from a bank? Why not learn to really love, to forgive, to unite, to be one with the universe and God?

For some reason, when we think about forgiveness and reconciliation, it seems we need to picture a crook, someone who harms or pains us deeply. True oneness and reconciliation reach further. Their scope is much greater. It is not a question of aches, but of the very essence of health and well-being. It is not a question of eliminating shadows; it is gaining light itself.

Reconciling is mercy itself. It is a manifestation of love and oneness. My God is merciful. We are truly lucky. A God that forgives the big and the small seventy-seven times, a God that is love. Love has enormous greatness, a power that cannot be measured.

There is a common belief that if one forgives and continues loving, one is stupid. We Christians, in whom the Spirit of Christ lives, have to turn that around. The truth is that if I do not forgive and love, I am stupid. I will deprive myself of life, light, peace, and God. I can be greater than my pride and my hurts. I can move in the movements of my God. This we have to experience, but we can experience it. Why not try and help one another to start using this beautiful and awesome sacramental power? For we are not the first: Jesus showed us how. It is easier than we think, it is mysticism. I never experienced more soothing and centering forces. They liberate from inner and outer divisions, they bridge every chasm.

"Father, may they be one in us, as you are in me and I am in you."(Jn 17:21.)

> Jesus, God, you live in me because you love me, you send me and bless me, you live for the total reconciliation of us all with you and the Father, you began it all: make me one with you. Unfold in me

the powers that you have given me, make me a rec-
onciler, a unifier, a movement of total love. Let me
be in you and with you that inner and total oneness
that you dreamed of and prayed for all of us. Help
me continue what you started. Make me in you and
with you a light, a vision, a hope, a sign, a path, a
movement that heals the world. Let us tell others
that they can be one as well, and that this oneness
is the joy of the universe. Thank you.

A movement is evident in the universe, in me, you,
and everything or everybody, towards a total union beyond boundaries of separation and difference. The one
and the whole are real, the oneness is a powerful process
to which I and all of us belong. It is my personal deepest
hope and that of mankind. There is nothing wrong with
dedicating my life to be what I see and what is to come.
It is very real and already possible in us.

Christianity in this sense can be understood as the
beautiful movement of becoming one, a reconciling force
given to us in the Christ-event, the forward movement
of being. Not just an ideal outside me or us, or a delusory
dream, but the very roots of being and joy. Such hope and
vision is part of the essence of individual and collective
life. The Christian therefore follows Christ as a liberator
from individualism and self-centeredness into the love,
union, greater order and wholeness. The total wholeness
is oneness with God and life beyond ourselves and time.
It is not outside us but very much within us.

Reconciliation is a creative power of life and love,
it is the prelude of total oneness.

The Power to Forgive

I have been forgiven by people and God, in the name
of God, by the church. That means loved, reunited, and
reconciled. It is a good feeling. It is good to receive love
and forgiveness, it heals, it activates again union and belonging. It makes real the bonding of oneness.

Beautiful though that be, another dimension of the Christian is perhaps as yet more beautiful. A Christian who lives in union with God and receives God's gifts, can forgive, can unite and reconcile. This is a gentle, overwhelming power. Mature love is always forgiving love.

Should we teach and instruct people to exercise the power that they have to forgive, that is to love as completely as God loves? "Your sins are forgiven," Jesus said to a paralyzed man; and of the unknown woman who washed his feet, he said "her sins, many as they are, shall be forgiven her, because she has loved much." (Lk 7:47.) Somehow, to do that requires the greatness of God. But it is such a joy of generosity and goodness to give forgiveness—love and union. Separating is always painful and it has undertones of death. Uniting and reconciling is always joyful and carries with it sounds of life.

God is love, therefore his mercy is boundless and he is always ready to forgive. The Christian, the person in whom God lives and who lives in God, shares in God's love and mercy; thus the Christian as well forgives always: always reconciles, always is peacemaker.

"My peace I give you." (Jn 15:27.) This is a reconciling gesture of Jesus. The Christian shares that power. He is a peacemaker and a peace giver. We have the power, freely given by our God to us his children, to be peacemakers, to love even when we are hurt or crucified, to reconcile and transform the universe.

This power is greater than the powers to be angry and take revenge, greater than nuclear destructive powers. Those powers may create more panic and fear; but life is greater than death, union greater than disunion. Without doubt, love is greater than hatred and more lasting.

We have been made to love rather than to hate. Why not activate such potential in us and enjoy it? Happiness increases in proportion with love and forgiveness. I know it in myself and others. And *vice versa*, hatred is like a cancer of the soul.

Since we have been made to love rather than to hate, why do we not dedicate schools to actualize and activate the unlimited power in people to love and forgive? We do that with lesser powers like job training and human skills.

Jesus developed the divine skill of reconciling God with us to the point of oneness, cosmic oneness. Forgiveness is an expression of the force and power of oneness. It is a mystical gift. Blessed are those who learn it and enjoy its practice.

Offertory

I find that we can live our lives in a liturgy of the living word, as the person of Jesus is and was a living word—much more complete than any written word. We can live in a sustained and sustaining process of offertory: recognizing what we receive from the Father—everything; blessing him for it; offering ourselves back to him in an actualization of our gratitude and his glory.

In this sense I like the words of the eucharistic offertory: "Blessed are you Lord of all creation, through your goodness we have this bread and wine to offer, fruits of the land, the vine and work of human hands, they will become our bread of life and spiritual drink." There is a beautiful emphasis on movements in "Blessed are you, through your goodness we have, we offer, they will become. . ."; this movement we will become. Should we confine these powers to recognize what we receive, to bless our God, and to offer to official movements or would we make them an attitude in our lives?

A few years ago I went back to my home country after a long and unplanned delay. The desire to return was intense. When I arrived in Madrid, I decided to visit some friends in the north, so I flew there. The welcome, the joy, the acceptance was overwhelming; it meant much to me. I was happy. I learned that other friends about one and a half hour drive away would also like to see me. Next morning, an early spring Sunday, I drove off to see these other friends. I was bouncing with joy; expectation, the life and light of a spring Sunday morning were filling me up and overflowing all of the vehicle. I did not know what to do with the feeling; it was intense, deep, high, and all-embracing. I looked at my God. He was there. I could not help saying to him "Thanks." That was not enough. He was happy making me happy. I decided that I had to do something with my joy, it was too much. So I took it and since my God was coming with me, I offered it to him as a gift of gratitude and blessing. He smiled, he took it, he was happy, he liked it. Since I noticed his pleasure, I gave him too the joy of my friends, those I left and those I was going to meet. He received that also gently and sacredly; as he was taking it, I still had it and my joy increased. I happened to look through the windows of the car and saw the light and colors of spring outside; the earth was joyful, pregnant with new life and freshness. Gently and sacredly I took all that, and recognized its beauty and blessings. I offered it to my God who was there with me. I knew that everything was coming from him and offering it back to him was a priestly duty of my faith and love. I did it, he accepted it without taking it away from me or from where it was. Once I started giving and offering, it was not easy to stop because it was a sacred movement which was uniting me with my God. It was fun, a silent conversation, very meaningful and very real. There were cows in the pasture, happy to eat a morning spring Sunday breakfast of fresh tender grass softened and decorated with dew and little flowers. I offered their joy to my God, they did not mind.

They were approving with the music of tiny bells hanging from their necks. Then I heard the birds singing. It was spring and the sun was bright and the birds were happy and colorful. I offered their joy and being, their songs, their presence and kindness in being with me on the road. They liked it and they approved. I knew it.

Suddenly I was in the town that was one and a half hours drive away. I thought that the drive took only about five minutes. I was enjoying the trip, and wanted to continue. I then realized that the trip was an offertory, a sacred giving back to my God what he was giving me. A meaningful movement of blessing and being blessed, it was a recognition of reality and a precious union with everybody and everything, mostly with my God.

Many times I have thought of that trip and shared it with others.

Should my life, our lives, be an offertory: a grateful recognition of the blessings we receive, even when we are in pain, and a sacred movement of giving back to our God what comes from him? I cannot tell you how centering and meaningful such a movement is; I only suggest you try and make it a constant directional way of being and self-giving. You shall sense a wholeness. It is deeply integrating.

The offertory of the Eucharist signifies and expresses the total offertory of our being, and unites us with the essential and total movement of Jesus, his self-giving to the Father in gratitude and love. This movement consecrates life and makes everything sacred.

Consecration

Sacredness is not boring. Somehow sometimes we are afraid of the sacred because of its depth; we might think of it as the opposite of the joyful. This is a widespread delusion. True, sacredness establishes a direction

of relating to life and curtails certain behavior as frivo-
lous or superficial. But it is not true that sacredness is
dull, unenjoyable or boring.

There is no substitute for the deep joy and happiness of being with a deep and reliable friend whose
friendship is so deep that it has become sacred. There is
no joy equal to the ecstasies one feels when surrounded
by the peaceful order of mysterious beauty, whether it
come from a person, an idea, a discovery, the mountains,
the flowers, the ocean or events that make one feel truly
blessed.

There is no well-being like feeling sacredly respected by people and life. Sacredness is an orderly connection and belonging to the sacred, to a greater majestic
and supreme being of life. Sacredness is at the core of
everything and every individual. Our connection with a
greater life is there—not that we make it, it is a given and
a gift, it relates to the very fact of being. We cannot make
it; we can discover it, accept it, share it, enjoy it, live it
and become in it.

That process of discovery, acceptance and proclamation is consecrating. It is an ordering and realistic
process. A movement of great wisdom. It is like entering
in a well-lit room where light eliminates fog and
shadows.

Sacredness and consecrating is a dimension of self-
identity and participation in the totality of existence.
Something like becoming a citizen: certainly, one as-
sumes burdens, and it is possible for one to focus on
them; but it is better to realize the privilege, the belonging, the sense of social wholeness, the strength of one's
fellows supporting one. So it is with sacredness: at the
heart of awe is a sense of existential wholeness, of mystical privilege, and of deep meaningful belonging.

Consecrating is a process of making something or
someone sacred. Now, as mentioned above, we do not

make sacredness, strictly speaking. We already are sacred. However, we can discover, enjoy, and celebrate the fact that we are sacred. Again, while in the deepest sense we already are sacred, at another level we can say that we make someone or something sacred when we unfold their sacredness and integrate it with the other dimensions of being such as awareness, emotions, relations, goals, and hopes.

In this sense, can I make myself sacred? Yes; I can discover the sacredness of my being and live it. This might sound too general and we can break it into parts. Can I make my time sacred or consecrate it? Yes; we all can. There is a sacredness in time, whether it is spent resting or working, talking or in silence, alone or with others. Drawing out such sacredness, being aware of it and enjoying it is to consecrate it. Can I make my friendships sacred? Yes; we all can. Friendship, when real and deep, is sacred; such should be the authentic direction of friendship. Friendship has a good, sacred joyfulness of belonging, loving and being loved, union, respect, and order. Those elements, when real and deep, point to and uncover the presence of the sacred, that is, of God; consequently, they imply sacredness. Can I consecrate my past, present and future? Naturally, it is like the sacredness of time.

What about pain, bad feelings and situations? There is sacredness even in death because it has a connection with life and God. Bad things can be transformed into good. Whether I am suffering or not, I am still sacred; in spite of partial evils, I can give my being a sacred dimension that in itself is a victory over evils.

In fact, when I realize the sacredness of the world and proclaim it, I consecrate the world. When I recognize and somehow signify the sacredness of another person, I consecrate that person.

Jesus consecrated himself in the fact of discovering, accepting and proclaiming his connection and oneness with the Father, recognizing that everything and everybody comes from and goes to God, his Father. The very movement of consecrating himself was his consecration of the world. Proclaiming and giving us the relation of sonship with God, he consecrated us. It was his priestly function.

Such movement and power we can exercise as well because it is in us. By the very meaning of Christianity, therefore, all Christians, who believe in and belong to Christ, are consecrators. People who in their very essence recognize sacredness and pertinence to God, people who translate such a recognition into expression and integrate their lives into sacredness make everything around and beyond themselves sacred. Such people are living fountains of meaning, dignity, respect, and joy. They enter into a new order and peace like the holy ones do, like Jesus did.

Communion

Communion alone unites, alone integrates. It is the movement that saves us from separation, isolation, selfishness, and death.

Jesus is the union and communion between God and man. No wonder that he signifies the movement with the sacrament of the Eucharist. "Amen, amen, I say to you, unless you eat the flesh of the Son of Man, and drink his blood, you shall not have life in you. He who eats my flesh, and drinks my blood has life everlasting. ... (Jn 6:54-55.) When he talked thus after the multiplication of the bread, many people left him. Either they did not understand or did not enter into the process of communion or oneness with him.

Do I want to? I will have to make my religion different from just ideas or human behavior. I will have to give my flesh and blood, all of myself to him and at the same time accept all of his. I will have to bow to a new identity in me, that of oneness, as Jesus said "I am in the Father and the Father is in me." (Jn 14:11.) Is that possible? It was for him and that is his wish: "He who eats my flesh and drinks my blood lives in me and I live in him." (Jn 6:56.) "Whoever lives and believes in me will never die." (Jn 11:26.)

How many times have I received the Eucharist? Many times throughout my life. Did I really reach through to the totality of communion? Did I become one with him? Not yet. Am I going to? Do I want to?

Communion takes more than receiving the Eucharist. Did I get involved in the sacred process that the Eucharist means? A little bit, yes. But am I going to stop there? How can I unleash that process so that I can reach the meaning and effects on total oneness?

It is a gift and a grace, but implies also a response. He is in me already and he has given himself to me, but have I given myself to him? I suspect that is the crunch.

The movement and possibility of communion, that is, of oneness with God is the greatest privilege for the human being. Intelligence could say that total dedication to that movement and the unfolding of such a gift should be the central endeavor of a spiritual man or any sensitive human.

How? I will search and try all means. It is an inward movement towards meeting my God, the risen Christ who lives in me and awaits me. The meeting, the acceptance, the inner embrace I know will produce new energy, light, life, being, a new me which would be me and he at the same time, one. ". . . I pray not only for these, but for those also who through their words will believe in me. May they all be one. Father, may they be one in us, as you are in me and I am in you, so that the world may believe it was you who sent me. . . . and that I have loved them as much as you loved me." (Jn 17:20-23.)

These words are real. We are called to the same union with Christ that he had with the Father. This is serious and beautiful.

The meeting point is me; it is in me where I will find and work out the oneness. As Jesus found the Father in himself, so in myself I can find the risen Christ and call him "Friend." The whole thing could be a dream and a bad delusion. I know it is not. It makes a good deal of sense. I feel it deeper than my bones. The whole reality of Christianity points to it.

Communion is a sacred movement of becoming one with my God and the universe at the same time. I do not want to let it go. It is a gift, a grace, and at the same time it is my self-giving.

It is a movement from God that needs a response from me. I suspect that is is easier than we think. "For anyone who wants to save his life will lose it; but anyone who loses his life for my sake and for the sake of the gospel, will save it." (Mk 8:35.) The paradox seems to apply well here. So my job and response would be the giving of myself to my God. Possible? Why not? Do we not give ourselves to things, events, people, and dreams?

I wonder if my life is going to change if I give myself in communion to my God. How can it not change? I long for the full realization of the oneness: finally I shall be. Even if I were to fail myself and my God, I would wish this realization for many: their joy of being would be total, the oneness would grow, the world would be God's light, beauty, and life will triumph because that is the one. This happened in Jesus and it can happen in us.

God, I know you want it. I know I have to put my two cents into it, I do want to. Bless me.

Movements of Gratitude

I try to imagine my life and my relationship with my friends without the movements—both ways—of gratitude and thanksgiving. I am very reluctant to imagine it: it would be my death. It is like imagining a child who cannot smile.

Gratitude as a movement has a unique beauty. I feel embarrassed and overwhelmed when I am grateful. I feel small, but I love it. I love it because I feel loved. And here is the center of its beauty : feeling loved. Gratitude accepts being loved and blushes back in love, with the gentleness of accepting one's limitations and needs; it is the beauty of interdependency that may grow into oneness. Expressed gratitude is a form of self-giving, appreciation, and love. Sometimes I find it is even more beautiful when unexpressed; it makes you mellow inside and awakens plenty of nice feelings. It becomes a responsive movement of harmony. I like its respect and the power it has to unfold cooperation. I will do practically anything for those to whom I am grateful.

When gratitude includes depths and lights, I mean when gratitude goes to boundless levels and becomes not a passing wind or an occasional breeze, but is bigger, like a consistent and permanent weather system, it creates a marvelous climate to be in. At these levels I am grateful to God not just for little favors but for my total existence, grateful for being in no matter what conditions, grateful for becoming, beyond time and before time. Thus gratitude makes a garden of my soul, humbleness and service grow naturally among other flowers such as generosity, appreciation; in the midst of them all is the joy of being loved.

This applies socially as well. How different is a group of people where gratitude—and the sense of being loved—flows horizontally, vertically and in all possible directions, from a group where ingratitude breeds distrust, resentment, selfishness, and isolation.

Jesus of Nazareth, I believe, lived in the movement of unrestricted gratitude to his God; he was aware that

God begot, blessed, and sent him: "This is my Son, the Beloved; my favor rests on him." (Mt 3:17.) And his gratitude to the Father was love returned. In Jesus I find the best summary of the most perfect movements of existing. His gratitude, like love, is somehow circular or spherical, not just unidirectional. Somehow love generates love, union generates union, and harmony generates harmony. There is nothing wrong in accepting that God the Father would move in gratitude towards Jesus, his Son, faithful, good servant, friend, responsive to the absolute blessing of sonship, unique messenger of grace.

I am grateful to Jesus of Nazareth for his unending light, for the grace and blessings that constantly I receive from him, for the modeling of being that he offers, for his call to the amazing opportunity to be one with him. He opens and offers the dimension to my life that makes sense. I am grateful to my God for his approaching movement of mercy, liberation, union, and life-giving. I am grateful. I feel blessed, and the feeling is real and natural. Ingratitude would be abnormal.

My gratitude as movement does not stop in my God; I am very grateful to many. I have received much. It is the joyful movement of being loved. Those who once loved—with the measure in which that was true—still love and value me, and they give what they gave, because those things which we are talking about are of a different nature. Those who once loved me still do whether they are aware of it or not because what I was given is still in me. I love in return, poorly though I express it. I am grateful and like to be so.

The Eucharist, of whose movements I have already written, a beautiful symphony of God's and human movements, would be incomplete if it ended without the allegro tones of gratitude and thanksgiving as the exultation of what it is and what happens in it. Gratitude is a natural outcome of well-being.

God, it is right and just that we give you thanks. I wish that the winds of gratitude would take over my land, my soul, and the land of mankind to the betterment of our gardens and for the unfolding of virtues that make you happy and give beauty to the face of the human.

Thank you God for being here, now, and always. I know that you are in me with great love. Thank you. Let my gratitude to you be a fertile river to refresh my life and those of others. Thank you.

Part 4

Psalms of Joy

Introduction

The Old Testament psalms are filled with
longing for God; these psalms respond to that longing
from the other side of the incarnation where we have
found the joy of discovering the living God. The movement of recognition, adoration, proclamation, order, relating to a higher being, sharing a discovery, serving as
a messenger.

The Joy of Glorifying

In a narrative in the gospel, Jesus goes for a retreat
to the desert for forty days and is exposed to evil temptations. This helps clarify the beautiful and centering
movement of glory. There Jesus is brought to the consid-
eration of the possibility of being adored himself, or
adoring evil and possessing glory and kingdoms. "I will
give you all these. . . if you fall at my feet and worship
me." He rejects that as a temptation and absurd, and re-

sponds: "Scripture says: You must worship the Lord your God and serve him alone." (Mt 4:9-10.)

It seems to be a common though often subtle temptation to aspire to be the center of the world, to need and want a disproportionate recognition and adoration. It is a delusion of being. Jesus in that situation pointed out and discovered an amazing avenue of wisdom: properly relating to a higher being, to the real and only God. It is the wisdom of the order that exists between the part and the whole. The wisdom of introducing in oneself the ability to relate to a greater truth, the awakening of the movements of awe, admiration, service, self-giving and proper belonging. As a lighter or a watch get meaning from relating to a higher being who created them to provide a flame or to measure time, so the human being gets existential meaning from properly relating to a higher being who created him or her for a purpose. Only in that relating will the purpose be found and developed.

"Father, glorify your name" (Jn 12:28): this is a movement of recognition. "I have made your name known to the men you took from the world to give to me." (Jn 17:6.) I wish that everybody would know you as I know you; that everybody would adore, respect, serve, relate to you as I do. This movement puts Jesus in a coordinate of truth with relation to himself, to his Father, and to the universe. So he will know where he stands, where he comes from and what his purpose in life is. On the other hand, those who never experienced the movement of true adoration would not know the immeasurable sense of peace and joy, the security and harmony that are felt while when adoring, the existential clarity and inner strength that comes from it, the meaning and sense it makes.

At first glance, there could be the delusion of thinking that by adoring and serving another being I diminish myself; in reality it is the opposite: only then do I truly be and become, because in that way I become part of the total being and one with my God, then is God in me and I am in him.

The recognition that God is fills much empty space of existence or life, because even if I were very big, I could never fill the universe; even a totally inflated ego does not fill much in this world. Merely to recognize and to accept that God is fill up the universe and make it possible to relate with him, set up a scenario of truth, put me in a realistic place, and provide a sense of plentitude and fulfillment. Recognizing God's presence is a movement which is already the beginning of prayer; it opens a door to adoration, acceptance, dialogue, love, and union. We lose much by consciously or unconsciously denying God's reality and presence.

"Father, glorify your name." Let everybody know that you are, and that you are present, and that without you there is no life, no being, no fulfillment; there is only an immense emptiness that nobody, no idea, no project can fill.

Glorifying God's name and presence is a movement of every valuing process. It certainly changes the direction of valuing from the self-glorification of the selfish and the proud to the glorification of God by the wise and the realistic. There is that unquestionable wisdom of Jesus when he directs and dedicates his life to glorifying the Father. Could I do the same? Indeed, not only can I, whoever I am, or wherever I might be, but that is the only path which will lead me to be, the only wise and sensible road of uniting with the whole. It would be ridiculous to live in the delusion of thinking of oneself as the center of the world, or even as the center of the country, or a city, or oneself, or thinking of oneself as the whole of being when one is just a part.

The movement of adoring God and recognizing him is as well the movement of finding purpose, of seeing the light, of being a servant and messenger, of carrying a mission. This is a powerful enlightenment and movement. For Ignatius Loyola, this summarized the project of his life and the dynamics of the religious order he founded. His motto was "To the greater glory of God." That enlightenment helped him choose, decide, inspire others and dedicate his existence to what he saw as the greatest purpose.

"Father, glorify your name." (Jn 12:28.) Not mine, but yours. Let me search for ways to make your name properly known; if people know you, they will love you, and give you the honor and recognition that is yours alone; not that I think you care about receiving honors and recognition as we humans do many times. But you know that if we knew who you are, and we recognized your presence, we certainly would be better off; a new dawn of peace and order would shine on us, we would be happy and one with you, we would enter into another type of life, eternal and heavenly, the life of total love. That is really what you want for us. If we only knew! I believe that you want the best for us, your children, and you have told us the way so clearly, so many times. Pardon our blindness, and please help us wake up, know you, adore you, and be one with you. Glorified be your name, in me and in everybody.

We could say much about the sacred movements of adoration and being sent and how they truly can benefit our being. This would be matter for an essay or treatise in itself. Here it might be enough to point it out; perhaps in another context, we can take up this subject as a style of life.

The Joy of Light

The light that enlightens the human being comes from the light. Light cannot come from darkness. The joy of being cannot come from problems, pain or any human darkness. There are great sources of light that enlighten humankind and happy are those who find them and have open, healthy eyes to see them.

There are ways to find the source of all light and meaning, which ultimately is God. Goodness is a path towards the light and so are humility, respect, prayer, meekness, and many other virtues. We can walk with them for miles and years until one day we find the light. The great joy then makes all the traveling indeed worthwhile. We all know the difference between being enlightened and living in darkness, and between artificial lights and the total light.

Light comes from outside, then dwells inside, and the inside is enlightened. I can be or perhaps am the dwelling place of the living God. If I truly believe, I have to say that I already am. So is every believer.

My light comes from God and stays with me and when it is in me I see. We do not see the light but in the light we see the dimensions and meaning of what is inside us. In the light of God, everything makes a different sense and it is easier to move around without bumping into obscure objects and feelings and without getting hurt.

I have walked in darkness and I know the difference from walking in the light.

We exist in the light and the light is with us but perhaps we must choose to accept it. Perhaps at times we are afraid of seeing in the light of God because we are afraid of truth and of finding out greater realities which would destroy our delusions. We cling to our delusions. One needs great humility, freedom, and courage to give up whatever delusions grow in one and to face humbly whatever truth the light manifests.

The mystics choose to live in the light, that light that comes from God and manifests the total truth. In the light they see the one and oneness. Then they lose the fear of being; the light of the true mystic bursts all his delusions; therefore, the perspective of the authentic seer is total reality, God, and he or she necessarily becomes humble. He or she cannot have delusions of grandeur, nor pride because he or she measures the self and everything else with the dimensions of the total reality that is God.

To accept the light and to live in the light is one of the greatest joys that a human being can experience. It is capable of producing ecstasies. Many mystics did and do live in the light.

Once I drove through the mountains in the middle of the night. I was alone, the road was narrow, winding, and unmarked. The fog was so dense that I could see only a few feet in front of the car. I could not see the road turning near the cliffs' edges. My fear was limitless. Then I found the taillights of another car and followed it for awhile. The people in the other car led me on my way. But their fear was greater than mine, and their pace much slower. So they gladly let me pass, and followed my taillights until many miles later we arrived at a small well-lit town. I stopped to rest and relieve my tension and fear. Those following my taillights stopped too for the same reason and thanked me for leading them. I thanked them too. The companionship helped all of us a great deal. We celebrated with dinner.

In daylight or with clear weather we would not have needed one another; neither would we have suffered that fear and tension.

At the inner levels of human existing, there are also mountainous roads, fogs, and unmarked roads. It is a joy to see the day coming, the fog lifting, the road signs, and taillights of other travelers.

Jesus of Nazareth, a human traveler, lived in the light; so well did he accept the light that he became the light and turned on the light for mankind. Even more he calls us to live in the light and to be light as well. That is why he said: "You are the light of the world." (Mt 5:14.)

It is a joy to turn on the light within people and to see them grow luminous.

Happy are those who believe, and open their inner eyes to the light of being because they will see clearly, they will avoid many fears and dangers, they will travel faster and more secure, and they will enlighten others.

The Joy of Peace

There is a story of a Chinese emperor who searched for peace and order with the neighboring kingdoms; unable to find a solution, he went to the mountain to seek advice from a wise man. The sage asked the emperor whether the peace that he looked for with the neighbors existed within the empire, within a province of the empire, in an imperial city, in a family or the imperial family, and, finally, within himself. That is all the sage said.

The joy of peace is the joy of order; any order, high or low, produces joy. Joy is the consequence of order and harmony.

The religious joy of peace comes from experiencing order of a very high quality: a sacred order with myself, others, with my God and consequently with the total being and the universe. This cosmic order can be achieved, and is enjoyable.

As a matter of fact, the unique sacredness of the quietness and peace of a holy person is that order. It talks by itself. It is like someone who has achieved the fullness of centering. The climate and atmosphere of order is within that person and emanates towards the outside, like a gentle, soft light.

When the feeling of being in place happens inside, the participation in a greater total order, the sense of a well-orchestrated movement, the quieting of the soul, awareness that one is a conductor of greater energies, all these and much more produce a truly indescribable joy in being. It is possible; religion is supposed to be the art of acquiring this feeling; in fact, Christianity is for those who discover it.

The joy of being at peace with oneself, with all of oneself, in the depths and in the shallows, and being at peace with all others, is not just an experience by the individual but is also shared. Have you ever felt the joy of total harmony and peace with a friend or group of friends? Then the circles of harmony and peace can expand. This shared experience is harmony and communication at levels greater or deeper than the merely verbal or physical. This experience of joy is there; we need not to prove it, for everyone has experienced it to a some extent and knows what I mean.

What does Christianity or religion have to do with it? Much. Christ is the one who talked about a new order, a total harmony, a loving and uniting with immeasurable dimensions, he is the one who could say throw me into destruction, disharmony and even death, and I will still be, because I exist in a new order. I am one with God and life.

Religion—Christianity in this case—if anything, has to be the art and process of ordering, and so it is. It unquestionably orders offenses by forgiveness, sin by grace, selfishness by charity, fears by trust, insecurities by the gentle and powerful security of a good God. Christianity activates and awakens the presence and gifts of a living God within the human being, orders the human with and within the divine, and establishes a new kingdom or order. Perhaps only the mystic begins to discover its joys, but then, we are all mystics. I wish I could unveil these realities to everybody; however, perhaps I can only try to enter them myself and cry out that they are there for everyone to enjoy.

The joy of order includes the order of thoughts, feelings, images, energy, things and people, friends and enemies, life and death, pains and pleasure. It is not idealistic, it is real, I know, and many I know experience it. There is a way: the way is a process and we are in it.

How could I explain it? Imagine a man who knows nothing about sailing or boating on the high seas with a rowboat or sailboat. Tell me about his fears, his being lost, the dangers that he runs, his panic and despair. Make him a sailor and watch how he orders the waves, the oars, the winds, the stars and takes a course. Naturally the metaphor is poor and incomplete, but it points out the direction of ordering. Our life is greater than the seas; our boat and soul is unsinkable, the winds are favorable and we have plenty of clear signs and stars to guide us; our landing in harbor is ensured.

The joys of ordering. I like to fix a watch and hear it tick, or a piece of machinery and see it move. Greater is the joy of tapping a human being in the right spot and seeing a smile, or the joy of coming out of my own clouds and seeing the sunshine, realizing that my life makes sense, that I am going, that I know where I am going, that the horizon is open and light, that there is order and God, and they are with me.

The joy of loving and uniting even with those I do not even know, or when I get nothing back: who cares about getting anything back? The joy is the loving and giving and ordering oneself, to the point of death if necessary.

The joy of being and ordering is like harmonizing with light. The light is already there, just open your eyes and see. Christianity is the light of God and life, and is there for those who want to see it, enjoy it and live in it. Is it hard or painful? No, in itself it is enjoyable, powerful, enlightening and life-giving. If by chance my eyes were bleary, that would be another question.

The Joy of Love

Much has been written about love and its many dimensions; it would appear to be superfluous to talk about the joy of love, which everyone knows about and has experienced. Yet I cannot ignore the important dimension which good, solid religion adds to love: it seems to me that, if people discovered this dimension, they would love more and better, and certainly would enjoy being loved much more.

In the minds and expectations of many, love has unfortunately been reduced to feelings and their physical manifestations. These are all right in their context, and it is not my purpose to attack them; rather, I would like to expand on the greatness and deep joys of the total phenomenon of personal love which makes anyone bloom.

Perhaps instead of using *love* we should use *union*, for it encompasses more and could include the whole being. We might use both. By *union* I understand a love that goes before and after feelings, above and beyond emotions.

I get great joy, for example, from being part of a group of people whom I respect and love, and among whom I am accepted and respected. It is most enjoyable to experience union and harmony among peoples, things, nature, music, art, and life. At times the experience follows being in love; other times the experience leads into and generates loving somehow.

True love respects and does not take advantage of people or things; in turn, a true lover of people and the universe generates back much respect for life. The atmosphere of respect is very enjoyable because of its security, its worthiness, its gentleness and because it is one of the greatest climates to be in or to grow in.

Religion, Christianity, has always had love as its center and basic law. I do not exaggerate if I say that

many of us at times were confused about a certain con-
tradiction in the way we struggle to love and to love well.
In my perception, for example, I was supposed to love
people, God, and myself with all my heart, energy and
soul. But I could not love particular individuals because
I feared there was sin in it; could not love myself because
I thought it was selfishness and therefore bad, and I did
not know whether or not I really loved God. So I was confused and afraid, unable to make a desired ideal into a
concrete reality.

I was trapped between the expansiveness of total
love—union with the universe—and the paralyzing fear
of doing wrong. The antimony made me crawl into a
hard shell. If I moved in either direction at the expense
of the other, I would pull my being apart either through
an unrealistic and inhuman idealism or through an
empty and gross humanism. For awhile I thought that
there was no solution and that I could only choose one
or the other. I felt a call to the desperate heroism of one
choosing one of the extremes. Somehow I was fixed in
the view that I could only go to the right or left. I was
forgetting that there are other axes of direction: a basic
up and down direction could integrate the right and left
extremes.

Joy broke in when, thanks to a more mystical vision
and sensation, I could look and experience the right and
the left from above—or beneath; the higher the point of
vision, the more united and closer right and left were and
both made sense. But their meaning had changed.

I can better illustrate what I am trying to say
through the gospel parable of the Good Father and the
Prodigal Son. In the story there is another figure, the
older son. For our purposes, we can locate the older son
in the extreme right horizontal. He represents loyalty,
hard work, ethics, practical love, faithfulness, reliability,
and responsibility. We can put the younger—the

prodigal—son on the extreme left horizontal. He would be the opposite: loose morals, sex, irresponsible adventurism, laziness, bad ethics, mismanagement and deplorable behavior. Both evaluations are true. Both would never get along and cannot be reconciled by themselves. Horizontally they separate. Only a vertical point can unite them and it does. From above appears the figure of the father in whom they unite, and both make sense. It is the high and deep love of the father that gives both of them a new dimension.

So it is with each one of us. When I experience myself from the dimension of good religion, that is, from God's dimension, my sins are forgiven and my righteousness is never enough. If I look at myself horizontally sometimes I am a sinner and other times a saint; I get confused. If I look at myself from the heights of God's vision, neither horizontal extreme is important; rather, the question is whether or not I come from God and go to God, that is whether or not I go up. If I take the verticality from beneath, what matters again is not right or left but depth or height, that is truthfulness, roots, becoming and the like. These are other parameters of relating.

What does all this have to do with the joy of loving? A great deal. If love is union and harmony, fanatic extremism will never get me to the joy of loving, or to loving in truth. Perhaps no linear movement would get me there. But if there are movements other than linear, like integrating and expansive movements, like the movement of love which is above sinfulness and human righteousness at the same time, which on one hand is at the heights of the spirit and at the same time at the depths of humanness? The movements of inflating or deflating a balloon are different than that of tracing a line from point A to point B.

The father in the gospel story is above the sinfulness of one son and the righteousness of the other. He rejoices in both sons; his joy is greater because his love is greater and he is both more ideal and more real than either of them because he incorporates both into him. Can I love at those levels? yes I can. Everyone can. Religion teaches me and guides me that way. It is not either/ or, but a new way of being, quite more complete and enjoyable.

Can you think of the joy of uniting what is divine and what is human and seeing that it works? Can you think of the joy of forgiving and the joy of being free from righteousness? The joy of loving like the mystics who find the connectedness of everybody and everything?

The joy of love is not the joy of possession or being possessed, although these can be temporarily exciting. The joy of love is the joy of union and harmony; when this union and harmony transcend ordinary levels of being and enter into existential, mystical levels, then it is incomparably greater. It acquires dimensions of freedom and security that the other levels do not know. In fact it harmonizes all levels of being, dissolves paradoxes, and unites all extremes. The ultimate joy of love, religious love, is entering into the total one and being part of it. It is seeing and feeling every exciting reality melting into one total reality. But do not think of this melting in physical terms, because physical diversity is an essential part of the mystical union. As a quite limited and faulty example, you can think of a perfect union and love between two people, say a man and a woman. Such a union, we all know, would not be just sexual, although sexuality can be an expression or part of it. Their souls click into oneness, not that they are exactly the same, but that they manage to form oneness complementing, interacting, fitting together, uniting. Their union covers the deeper dimensions of being human. The greater the union at the core of being, the greater room and freedom there is for diversity at other levels such as physical, emotional, intellectual, occupational, and so forth. The more love is restricted to these other level, the less freedom and respect they would enjoy even at those levels. That clearly is the cause for jealousy and possessiveness.

Without doubt, good religion develops love at the core of being, love that is real, concrete, and yet without physical, emotional and intellectual boundaries. It is joy when one is able to experience love without boundaries. If people only knew.

The Joy of Inner Order

From disorder come much pain, stress, frustration, and despair, especially when the disorder is deep in the existential levels of the person. Likewise, much joy comes from inner order, when existentially one knows one's place, direction, mission, goals, and where one belongs, and what resources are available.

A great advantage of the Christian religion is that in Christ everything is ordered, for he was and is the living unification of the universe and the mysterious universal forces that exist in each individual. Christ is the totality of meaning because in him the divine is ordered with the human. He ordered himself towards God and towards men properly and at the same time. In him I find the answer to my being, to where I come from and go to, to what to do with thoughts, emotions, aspirations, inner and outer being. He is the image of my evolution and the evolution of mankind. We evolve towards a new spiritual existence which is beyond time and physical space.

When Jesus says: "my peace I give to you" (Jn 14:27), he probably was playing on the fact that *shalom* was the ordinary everyday greeting and farewell among his people. The prophet Jeremiah said that everybody is going around saying "Peace, peace" while betraying one another (Jer 6:14, 8:11; *see also* 9:8). In Christ the word *peace* now is true, fully real; he gives that total transcending order which in turn gives meaning, hope and life to being.

When I can put my past in harmony and order with my future, my outside human world with my inside spiritual world, my body with my soul, my friends with my enemies—that is, put sense in my contradictions and paradoxes, then I will be in order or at peace. As a human task it seems impossible, but since the order is already there, I can allow it to happen.

It is the wisdom of balance, an equilibrium between activity and passivity, joy and pain, talking and listening, loving and being loved, giving and taking, searching and believing, living and dying.

There is a joy in the deep existential order of being. God is that order: in him the opposites meet and converge; in him death ends and life begins; in him despair becomes hope; confusion changes into meaning, weakness into strength, darkness into light, the human blossoms or resurrects into the divine, time melts into eternity. In and at the touch of God the old man becomes a child, and sterility revives in fertility. All this is a joy to experience and watch.

The Joy of Blessing and Being Blessed

Religion in itself is a blessing; but by its very nature, it overflows in all directions with blessings.

Blessing is an expression of good wishes, a special favor granted by God, anything that contributes to holiness, or an approbation of goodness. By such a standard, religion is an overwhelming blessing. But further, it is a channel to bless and be blessed.

The blessings I have received and give through my religion are countless. Because through religion I know God, this knowledge increases the happiness and stability of my whole being. Accepting the reality that God raised to the status of his child is an immeasurable joy. Sharing my faith, hope, and union with others unfolds and increases my being and joy. That I can be and am a blessing to others, that I can actually bless others is a joyful privilege. This privilege is not reserved to the ordained priest; all Christians can share and distribute Christ's blessings. As a matter of fact, the main business of the Christian is to distribute and share blessings. There is no doubt that Christianity is a blessing to mankind, to you and me, and to those who are open to be blessed.

What a joy if my life would just be a blessing to myself and to others and to my God.

Blessing is basically a movement of communicating goodness, love, support, life, and joy. I am blessed in my friends. When I think and feel that God has blessed me, I recount or bring into presence the good things that come to me from my God. When I bless people and my friends, I give them the best I have: the inner sacredness which comes from my God and mysteriously dwells in me.

When the angel blessed Mary, he announced God in her. When Jesus blessed the apostles, he gave them his peace and powers, he gave them himself, and he gave them the Holy Spirit.

We all can bless, a truly sacred movement. Blessing is a giving movement. Being blessed is a receiving movement. Sometimes I feel the flow of the blessing powers coming in and out of me like the light flows through crystal.

I pray to be a blessing to all those who come in touch with my life. Sometimes I know that people coming in

contact with me have suffered because of me or because
of themselves, because of life, or because of meaningless
chance events. They are in the forefront of my blessing
desires, and I believe that they are blessed, and that God
answers my prayers.

Jesus was a man who passed through life blessing
and his blessings were effective. I hope I can do the same;
if my union with my God is pure and humble, my blessing
will be effective.

> God, let my life be a blessing for many, those
> I love most and all those whose lives I have touched;
> let my life be blessing for you and your people and
> creation. Bless me, Father, in your love.

The Joy of Staying with God

When I feel bad as well as when I do feel good, I can
stay with God in me, around me and beyond me. Relating
with others, for business or for pleasure, in depth or in
superficialities I can stay with God in me, in them, in the
middle and beyond.

In sickness or in health, I can stay with God and rest
in him, and let him rest in me.

To stay with God: to stay with the ineffable meaning of being, with dimensions and perspectives beyond
what is grasped. It is to defy loneliness, emptiness and
uselessness. It is to allow the continuity of believing, loving, and hoping. It is to exist in the oneness which overflows and extends beyond one's perceived or experienced
existence. Staying with God is staying with being, with
life, with oneness, with love, with peace, with the eternal.

Staying with God is different from action,
thoughts, words, or other human movements. It is beyond and can include all those movements. Staying with
God is in fact the eternal task of being. It is the greatest
and most secure source of peace and order. It is an actualization of faith because it is honoring and accepting

God's reality and presence and embracing that reality and presence. It is an actualization of love, because it unites. It is an actualization of hope, because God always stays with us—me—through inner valleys and mountains, through any kind of feelings and moods, through all those growing human pains and joys. He is faithful and loving, staying with me—us.

The fourth gospel says that the Word, who was always with God, and was God, "was made flesh, he lived among us," or "he pitched his tent among us," and we saw his glory . . . as the only Son of the Father. . . . (Jn 1:14.) That tent, the dwelling place of God, fulfills the Old Testament figure of the Tent of Meeting, the shekinah or presence of the Lord and his glory. This presence is an essential part of God's covenant with his people, and is fully realized at the end of the world. Another writing from the Johannine school, *Revelation*, describes this in the figure of the new Jerusalem:

> Then I heard a loud voice call from the throne, "You see this city? Here God lives among men. He will make his home among them; they shall be his people, and he will be their God; his name is God-with-them. He will wipe away all tears from their eyes; there will be no more death, and no more mourning or sadness. The world of the past has gone." (Rv 21:3-4.)

There is an eternal commitment, unbroken by God, and renewed when we fail. That is God's sacred covenant of staying with us.

The Joy of Conversion

The immense joy of conversion comes from a change of center of consciousness, which implies more than a change of direction. Look at St. Paul. His new center is Jesus and his resurrection. This means that he has new life, new vision, new energy generated by the very process of proper centering. Jesus was always centered in the Father, was one with the Father. From that centering and oneness emerged unmeasurable life in him.

The unconverted is the selfish one; the worst center for a human being is the self.

For us, the center towards which we convert is Jesus, the resurrected Jesus who cannot be separated from the Father and the Spirit.

I see conversion as a centering process and movement; in as much as it is centering and consequently harmonizing, it is one of the deepest, most joyful processes or movements of being. It cannot be reduced to an act, though it is manifested in acts and actions.

We all search for centering and conversion, the joyful experience of union; naturally, the more we unite within, the greater the joy. If we achieve the union beween God and us, the union is totally redemptive and salvific.

Sinfulness is from this point of view the opposite of conversion.

The Joy of Serving

Sometimes I have been in charge of things and in our small way of thinking, of people. In reality, we are never in charge—although sometimes we take a joy in the delusion of power, the sense of achievement, the impression of authority, and so forth. However I never enjoy that as much as when I was doing a service to someone I loved. There is such a unique joy in giving of oneself through service to those one cares for that wisdom would say that one of the greatest paths to joy is humility and service, and that the wise one is a servant.

Here the thinking of religion and the religious differ widely from the common delusion that dominating, controlling, being above others, being served are the greatest joys. Experience tells me that the joy is greater

in freely serving. It is not dominating or being domi-
nated, it is freely giving and taking, uniting in freedom,
making the other feel important, valuable, good, worthwhile and sacred. It is not being above or beneath, but
being one; joy comes from harmony, and there is great
harmony in serving and being servant to others. Jesus
said: "the Son of Man has not come to be served but to
serve" (Mt 20:28).

To serve God we serve people, a community and
mankind. There is a joy in it and we can serve from any
position of life, from any status, by simply offering and
giving what we are and have. If we all could share this
attitude, slavery would be eradicated. It is a form of in-
corporating oneself into a higher being, so that all together form a new total, a more complete body.

The Joy of Spiritual Receiving

Why is it that I am more aware of what I give to God
or religion than of what I receive? I would like to open
the doors of my receiving, spiritual and human.

Perhaps, inside, I overvalue what I give—
surprisingly I often am not aware either of what I mean
to others or what I really give—and my awareness of
what I receive is very limited. I am aware of what I receive
materially or physically. Sometimes too, of the love, af-
fection, and respect that I receive. But I am not aware of
how much God loves me, that he really trusts me and enjoys me. I am not aware or do not experience that God
likes me, and that many people like me. I know that I
want to be good and be close to my God but do not experience that my God likes to be with me, in me, that he enjoys it, wants it, and that he always wanted to be in me.

I do not experience it, but I believe it. I am trying
to open the doors of my receiving. The awareness of receiving, the opening and humility to receive is joyful, is
peaceful, is life-filled, is lightsome, and it leads me to re-

ceive myself and from myself. This does not make me
selfish or self-centered, because when it is true, it generates beautiful movements of spontaneous giving and
sharing.

Guide me, God, to receive humbly and grate-
fully, to receive from you, and from others, to receive you and others with open doors; then I shall
have more to give because I will give myself but inside me—that new me—will be a blending of you,
others and me. Then I will give a mysterious one
where we will not be divided but all united in a
powerful and enjoyable oneness.

Guide me, God, to manage my expectations
and to know what to receive, to welcome goodness
and beauty from everybody, even when I do not see
it. For I receive you constantly through and from
others, in all sorts of manifestations. Teach me to
receive when I give and to give when I receive so
that both movements blend into one reality and a
joyful living.

"He came to his own and his own received
him not. But to as many as received him he gave
the power of becoming sons of God." (Jn
1:11-12.)

God, you are coming to me constantly in different forces, through different people. I know. Let
me receive you, in them through them. I will become your child, your light, your glory, your epiph-
any, your peace, your joy. Thank you.

The Joy of Receiving

We are made to be receptive. Perhaps we become
what we receive, and our receptivity has much to do with
the processes of becoming and the result of our being.

Those who receive God have the power of becoming
children of God, one with God, an expression and epiph-
any of their God, Word of God, temples of the living God.

The fire receives wood or oil and fire becomes alive;

the wood is transformed into light, warmth, power, and new energy, an expansive movement. When that fire receives water a process is stopped, or put out. This is a simple image. When I receive God, a process of light, a new movement and life happen within me that are expansive.

We are truly receptive. Much comes to me through the eyes, through my mouth, my ears, my sensing, my mind, my heart. Often I have a choice of what to eat, see, hear, sense, and love. How could I keep my receptivity doors open to what is good and closed to evil?

Jesus of Nazareth was a man open to good and God and closed to evil. He was open to truth and closed to hypocrisy and lies. Open to mercy and compassion and closed to egoistic selfishness, open to union and love and closed to separation and stifling structures. He was totally open to life and closed to death. Open to light and closed to darkness. Can we be like him? To be like him is the task of the consecrated individual, an exercise of receiving. It is the art of knowing what to receive and thus a concrete way of becoming. How much can I receive? I can receive God and goodness constantly. Then, I will have something to give.

Thank you God for making us receptive and for the reality of Jesus.

The Joy of Silence

There is joy in looking at a flower and saying nothing, in listening to the songs of the birds; there is joy in looking at the sky and seeing the clouds, and in flying over the clouds in airplanes; there is joy in saying nothing, just seeing and listening, and wondering, and being with. There is joy in looking at people with respect and letting them be and saying nothing. There is joy in connecting with others, with animals, with mountains and rivers and God, and saying nothing, just looking, accepting respecting, letting be. There is joy in letting my hand be without twisting it or forcing it, joy in gently touching a stone, a tree, a pet, a person. Joy in silence, in saying nothing. There is a paradoxical joy in accompanying someone in pain or struggle, saying nothing, just being with. There is a joy in listening to the airplane, the wind, the water and the passing by of humans in the rapids of life. There is joy in silently giving, helping, receiving, being with the seasons of life.

There is joy in silence, and I am not talking about mutism or dumbness, but about wisdom, admiration, wonder, respect, sacredness and another level of communication deeper than words and noises. There is a cosmic stereophonic sounding of the universe for those who can unplug the ears of their being.

I love to listen in silence to the joys of people, to their worries, to their life stories, and the noise of things. Perhaps listening is a way of ordering. I can hear birds and people, automobiles and machinery, I can hear the harmony of people, I hear search and joy of those who find. I hear God and the Spirit.

There is a beauty in silence, and the joy of admiration, of respect, of dignity, of accepting and self-giving, and in it too, there is a plentitude of expression.

> Lord, I want to be silence like You are.
> The silence that says everything, that is to say,
>   that says Presence, Truth, and Peace.
> Silence of adoring, not silence of having
>   nothing to say.
> Silence of closeness, not silence of distance,
> Silence of love and respect, not the one of fear
>   or despite.
> Silence which would be the climax of saying
>   and expressing, like Yours.
>
> The silence of the mountain and the flower,
>   of the sun and of life, which is the plentitude

of being, the plentitude of self-giving and the
dedication to simply be what one is.

Lord, let my silence be You, a constant
    and profound
Yes, filled with peace and truth.

Silence of living with an inner smile.
Silence of understanding and accepting.
Silence of praying and adoring.
Silence of well-being and walking along
Silence of giving without asking why.
Silence of humility, of being and saying nothing.

The Joy of Religion

Religion is a discovery of beauty, truth, light, life,
meaning, being and much more: it is a discovery of God
and oneself. The discovery of such realities can only be
overwhelmingly joyful. Religion consequently is the excitement of search plus the joy of discovery. It is like a
fisherman who after many predawn hours without any
catch suddenly finds an enormous bank of fish and fills
his net up almost to the breaking point.

It is like a buyer who searches for years for something he always wanted and suddenly comes across it,
even better than expected, and at half price.

It is like a sick person that after many years of pain,
medicine and limitations finds a cure, feels wholeness,
and begins to function well.

It is like peace after war.

It is like a person who has suffered loneliness and
rejection for a long time and then finds a true friend and
begins to love.

Religion is the joyfulness of encountering light in
darkness, of becoming alive after a long death.

It is a gift from the God of being who has already
given the treasure now hidden within us; there is an art

in discovering it. Jesus of Nazareth discovered that God was his Father and lived within him, that he had divine powers and nature, that he himself was the light, the truth and the way.

People whom we call mystics discovered that everything makes sense within an ineffable connection with one God, and that everything is part of a whole; they sense and enjoy the harmony of oneness. When human beings discover that God is in them and they in God, religion—union—happens as a joyful event.

To discover divinity within us is a joy given us freely, a gift of our God giving himself to us. If we accept, we can become children of God, heirs of God, one with him, the family of God, with a right to live forever. Quite a bit more than a sweepstakes or a lottery prize.

Religion is the joy of such discovery. The one who finds it could care less about many other things. As Jesus said, one would sell everything to have such treasure.

It is a joy to discover oneself in those inner connections with God and others, with unsuspected beautiful dimensions of being and belonging, and a joy to share it with others so that they can find it too. Jesus' discovery of his sonship and his sharing it with us transformed mankind.

To discover who we are and God living within is not difficult. It would be difficult, even impossible if we would have to make God or our being in relationship with him. But we do not have to make such realities, they already are, offered freely to us. It is easy to enter into a building through the door with the right key. That is what doors are made for. There are certain attitudes which are the key for the experience of encounter and discovery about which we are talking. Such are humility and a sense of truthfulness, the childlike simplicity of nonjudgment in faith and belief, the sense of wonder and admiration, the receptivity and gratitude of needing, the

openness to unity and love, the simplicity and spontane-
ity of self-giving, the simplicity of doves and the pru-
dence of serpents. These things come naturally to the
human being. Unfortunately we can build walls around
ourselves, such as pride, stupidity, distrust, selfishness,
and other defenses that block the door of communicating with the depth of us and others.

The message of Jesus of Nazareth, his attitudes, his
teaching is the path to discovery; its clarity and simplicity are as great as its depth and beauty. Jesus compared
religion—the kingdom and reign of God—to the joys of
a banquet, the finding of what was lost, the unearthing
of a unique treasure, the festive welcome back at the
house of the Father.

The business of religion is the art of making all
these things personal experiences and enjoying it. If any
small price is necessary for the process, it is very much
worthwhile.

The Joy of Being Cared For

A religious person, that one who has faith, knows
and feels that his God takes care of him. For many years
in religion I was eager to take care of learning, praying,
giving, serving, and growing. I read many times in scripture that God takes care of his people. I never deeply
experienced being taken care of by God. On many
occasions I felt God's providence, but also felt that
I would be superstitious if I accepted a personal
caring.

But now it is hard to deny a personal caring and protection from my God. It is more than a guiding hand. I
receive much. The caring comes at many levels; the less
important and most superficial one is the physical—
surprisingly this level most often is the most noticeable
and relevant for us. Then there is a psychological one,
and there are deeper ones, those of the spirit, of life that

is eternal, of essence of being, belonging, levels of being born into a God.

The feeling of being cared for is an ineffable warmth, is humbling and yet it really brings a tender security and joy, a call for response and love.

The Joy of Having a God

Probably those who have no God would not know the joy of having a God. It is an immense joy to have a God who is always accepting and forgiving, a God as a companion, as a Father, as protector and a guide, a God who is a refuge, who provides, who loves totally, who is real and is always there.

It is joyful to know God, to dialogue with him, to be in him and with him. What would I be without my God? Where would I go without him? My God gives meaning and direction to my life and my total being. I would be empty without God. Sadness would shadow my life.

It is a joy to have a God to search for, to discover while evolving towards him, to tell everything to, to hope for and believe in. Still it is a greater joy knowing that God is true and is here and lives in me.

It is a joy to serve my God and love and unite with him. There is a joy in knowing where I am coming from and where I am going to, to know that I do not exist in a vacuum, that I am part of a total being, that there is a direction in my existing and the direction is good.

The Joy of Being

Practically we are all afraid of not being. Everybody likes to be. This is what the following mean: "they do not like me," "I have no place to go or be," "I am nobody," "I failed," "I fear rejection, sickness, death, certain situations." It is a basic fear of not being. On the contrary, when people say "I earn a big salary," "I am a star, a

102 GOD WITHIN US

success," "They expect me," "I have all that I want,"—
theseare expressions or signs of being. There is great
hunger to be and many times if we are not, we manage
to fake it and try to give the impression to ourselves
and others that we are. We all know there is a whole
lot of faking going on.

Can we really be without faking? Can we ensure it?
We can. Then there is no need to boast or fake, but just
enjoy that one is. The interesting thing is that we already
are and we only need to discover it: that is what religion
does for me, and I constantly experience that it does to
many others who search and want to discover themselves. This is not empty drivel. The human being has
riches inside which only can be grasped, shared and discovered through good religion. When that happens, the
need to fake that we are disappears. Naturally the one
who really has, does not need to boast about it.

It is sad to have things and not to have ourselves.
It is sad that we value structures, machines, ideas, other
people, buildings, publicity, images—and we do not
value ourselves. Why not discover who we are, and measure ourselves with proper measures of being, instead of
constantly putting ourselves down? Good religion is a
way of doing that, of finding that we are and enjoying it.

Often we believe that we are what we do, what we
have, or part of the organization that we belong to. Religion tells us and proves that we are more than that. It
affirms and develops the spiritual dimension of being,
the divine dimension of being and consequently en-
riches tremendously the identity of a person. We still
own the other partial identities and integrate them into
a total identity and a more powerful sense of being. For
example, a traveler considers his or her nationality important or rather essential. It means roots and protection; that sense of nationality or citizenship integrates
one's other identities, like what he or she does, has,

knows, feels, searches for, and so forth. Still a deeper rooting and existential protection and identity is what a good religion offers. Belonging to a God, being sent by a God, coming from a God and going to that God, having that God inside and ordering into that God one's thoughts, feelings, actions, goals and relationships, provides the person with a type of identity which is so securing, peaceful, empowering, and liberating, that a sense of being anew, everlasting and alive, will permeate such a person. This person will just enjoy being and knows and experiences that he or she is.

Today for many being is quite stressful and even agonizing because of confusion, despair, and inability to cope. The one who is religious has a new weapon to liberate oneself from stress, despair, and disorder. Religion makes one's being meaningful by providing an order beyond one's own boundaries and beyond society's boundaries. It gives a transpersonal and transsocial harmony which is an enjoyable peace. It opens the horizons of life and offers constant, realistic hopes, so that there is no longer a feeling of being lost or at an existential dead-end road.

Then, the connection with other human beings becomes existential and not just temporary. Many fears—fears of emptiness, fears of not being—deeply seeded within us will disappear, as darkness disappears when the sun comes up into the day. Then being is enjoyable.

I can experience in good religion that I am important to my God, to others and myself, and I am not just saying comforting words, I am talking about experience. Religion, good religion, is supposed to make us feel good, not miserable, should create a sense of worth and well-being because it introduces us to levels and depths of love unknown to the irreligious. The deep joy of self-acceptance and the calm sense of secure being of a centered religious person are worth searching for and are attainable, easily attainable with a bit of guidance from an experienced master.

The advanced religious person, the mystic, would achieve such heights of being, and would find himself so connected with the total being that he or she would say with St. Paul "I live now not with my own life, but with the life of Christ who lives in me." (Gal 2:20.) Paul expresses a unique, powerful oneness, the blending of his being with the being of Christ. That connectedness with the total being is a call and a gift to all of us. In fact, we are already connected and we only need to discover it, and becoming aware of it accept it as a reality in which we exist. It is a most enjoyable dimension of any human.

Perhaps the mystics are those who better grasp that joy of finding everything and every moment connected with the oneness of the total being; but then, we are all mystics to a certain degree, like we all have the ability to see and hear; what remains is only the question of how we develop these abilities. Good religion, again, will lead us into new mystical perceptions of self and the world, into proper connectedness with the mystery of being and God.

I believe that there is a joy of being found through religion that cannot be attained otherwise, not through philosophies or simple humanism and certainly not through ignoring or denying the most dignified dimension of a person which is one's spirituality.

The process of spiritual growth in the individual does not at all impair other human growth in the person; on the contrary, it enhances, invigorates and integrates it.

No career, no job, no possessions and no training could have given me a deeper and more balanced sense of being than that which religion gives me, in my case, Christianity. In Christ is where I really am. Christ, the result of Jesus of Nazareth being one with God, resurrecting and opening for all of us the possibility of being children of God, being one with him, of God being alive in us and us in him, Christ, the phenomenon of a new total being, the total body of believers. It is in him that any being, as that of everyone who wishes it, takes a new light and a bigger than cosmic dimension beyond time and space. What I say is not dreaming or simple poetry or idealism, it is an experiential reality available for those who want it.

Because of Christ I am more and I am total, with him and through him I connect with the universal and eternal being, and I belong to a new wholeness. The expansive force of God or Christ in me is immeasurable, the bonds with life and in it with people and the universe are so gentle and powerful that if unleashed, I feel, would put us in such a state of elation that we would burst. In him resurrection would be inevitable.

We cannot be backwards. That is to say, the human being cannot grow in being by regression towards what is less, like an unintelligent animal or machine, or an object, or lifeless matter. No, humankind to be has to go forward, to another being or state of being more intelligent, loving, perceptive, sensitive, spiritual. We can only move in the path of becoming towards God or better said, towards the one God. How can I have a sense of being and becoming if I move backwards or give myself to what is less that I am? There is only one path of growth and greater being for the human and that is God's life. It has been promised and it is attainable. The intelligent human being would launch himself in that direction to be, towards the joy and excitement of God's life.

Just Be

Just be.
Let the people be.
Let the waters run and the flowers grow,
Let the mountain stand
    and the valley sleep.
Do let everybody be,
Let the squirrels play
    and the turtles love,
Let the stars be quiet,
Let the dreams pass by.
Just be.
Let the music sound
    and the peace take over.
Just be.

Conclusion

Question: Lately, have you seen the face of the living God—that is the resurrected Christ who did not die forever, who is still alive and lives among us?

The answer of many would be: No. Are you crazy?

We see the face of money, the face of buildings, cars—and we know their names—things that we like, people, earthly humans, ... we see the face of pains, problems, illnesses, tragedies, death. . . but God? Who can see the face of God? Perhaps only angels can see the face of God. We must be realistic.

Let me ask again.

Have you seen the face of life coming? Have you seen the smile of a baby that mysteriously comes to life and grows? Have you seen deep joy?

Have you seen the trees and flowers that stubbornly open up every year?

Have you seen the overwhelming power and order of life in the forest? Have you seen life moving?

If you peek through that, you might see the face of a God that is life, who creates and gives life.

Have you seen love? And do not tell me that true love does not exist or is not real. If you look closely, you might see the reflection of the face of a God that is love, deep oneness that is.

Have you seen goodness in people and in yourself? Do not tell me that there is none. There is much. Just look at it, you will see the face of a God that is Good. The beauty of goodness can only originate in a God. Have you seen people who are generous, self-giving, forgiving, respectful, sacred? If you have not, perhaps you were looking in the wrong direction. Please look properly. Do not say that they are not.

If you see them, or that in yourself, perhaps you are seeing a sign, a manifestation—a face—of a living God, who is alive and dwells in us.

Have you seen lately the face of the living God?

I tell you, when you see it, your heart will jump in joy. There is life and there is hope. When you see it, your inner self will smile from within like a morning, your feet will grow wings to move towards him, your eyes will sparkle with the plentitude of discovery and wonder. Your ears will listen for the sound of his silence.

When you see it, you will become alive and if you keep looking you will never die.

Have you seen the face of the living God? The resurrected Christ who did not die forever, who is alive and lives in us?

When you see him, please believe, he is here. He came back. He never left us. With him and in him we are all one.

Index of
Scriptural References